AND THE WALLS CAME TUMBLING DOWN!

THE RISE AND DEMISE OF THE CATHOLIC CHURCH IN 20TH-CENTURY IRELAND

EILEEN MCCOURT

And the Walls came Tumbling Down!

By Eileen McCourt

This book was first published in Great Britain in paperback during August 2024.

The moral right of Eileen McCourt is to be identified as the author of this work and has been asserted by her in accordance with the Copyright, Designs and Patents Act of 1988.

All rights are reserved, and no part of this book may be produced or utilized in any format, or by any means, electronic or mechanical, including photocopying, recording or by any information storage or retrieval system, without prior permission in writing.

All rights reserved.

ISBN: 979-8336092844

Copyright © August 2024 Eileen McCourt

CONTENTS

About the Author i

Acknowledgements x

Foreword xi

Chapter 1: The institutional nature of the Catholic Church 1

Chapter 2: All God's Men! Irish and Catholic synonymous - how did that happen? 11

Chapter 3: Society in 20th-century Ireland: the image and the reality.. 48

Chapter 4: '*Bless me Father*!' - Being a good Catholic - 20th century Irish-style! 65

Chapter 5: The long tentacles of the Catholic Church in 20th-century Ireland 70

Chapter 6: The winds of change begin to blow 77

Chapter 7: And the walls came tumbling down! 99

Epilogue: The Catholic Church in modern Ireland 123

Bibliography 131

Other Books by Eileen McCourt 133

About the author

Eileen McCourt is a retired school teacher of English and History with a Master's degree in History from University College Dublin.

She is also a Reiki Grand Master teacher and practitioner, having qualified in Ireland, England and Spain, and has introduced many of the newer modalities of Reiki healing energy into Ireland for the first time, from Spain and England. Eileen has qualified in England through the Lynda Bourne School of Enlightenment, and in Spain through the Spanish Federation of Reiki with Alessandra Rossin, Bienstar, Santa Eulalia, Ibiza.

Regular workshops and courses have been held in Elysium Wellness, Newry, County Down; New Moon Holistics N.I. Carrickfergus, County Antrim; Angel Times Limerick; Holistic Harmony Omagh, County Tyrone; Celtic School of Sound Healing, Swords, County Dublin; Reiki Healing Bettystown, County Meath and Moonbeams, Carrigaline County Cork, where Eileen has been teaching the following to both practitioner and teacher levels:

- **Tibetan Usui Reiki levels 1, 2, 3 (Inner Master) 4 (teacher) and Grand Master**

- **Okuna Reiki (Atlantean and Lemurian)**

- **Karuna- Prakriti (Tibetan Usui and Hindu)**

- **Rahanni Celestial Healing**

- **Fire Spirit Reiki (Christ Consciousness and Holy Spirit)**

- **Mother Mary Reiki**

- **Mary Magdalene Reiki**

- Archangels Reiki
- Archangels Ascended Masters Reiki
- Reiki Seraphim
- Violet Flame Reiki
- Lemurian Crystal Reiki
- Golden Eagle Reiki (Native North American Indian)
- Golden Chalice Reiki
- Golden Rainbow Ray Reiki
- Goddesses of Light Reiki
- Unicorn Reiki
- Pegasus Reiki
- Elementals Reiki
- Dragon Reiki
- Dolphin Reiki
- Pyramid of Goddess Isis Reiki
- Kundalini Reiki
- Psychic Energy Surgery Healing

Details of all of these modalities can be found on Eileen's website, together with dates and venues of courses and workshops.

This is Eileen's **50th** book.

Previous publications include:

- **'Living the Magic'**, published in December 2014
- **'This Great Awakening',** September 2015
- **'Spirit Calling! Are You Listening?',** January 2016
- **'Working With Spirit: A World of Healing'**, January 2016
- **'Life's But A Game! Go With The Flow!',** March 2016
- **'Rainbows, Angels and Unicorns!',** April 2016
- **'........And That's The Gospel Truth!',** September 2016
- **'The Almost Immaculate Deception! The Greatest Scam in History?',** September 2016
- **'Are Ye Not Gods?' The true inner meanings of Jesus' teachings and messages',** March 2017
- **'Jesus Lost and Found',** July 2017
- **'Behind Every Great Man........ Mary Magdalene Twin Flame of Jesus',** July 2017
- **'Out of the Mind and into the Heart: Our Spiritual Journey with Mary Magdalene',** August 2017
- **'Divinely Designed: The Oneness of the Totality of ALL THAT IS',** January 2018. Also in **Audiobook**, May 2019
- **'Resurrection or Resuscitation? What really happened in That Tomb?',** May 2018

February 2022

- *'You're just a number....and the Universe has it!'*, May 2022

- *'Let Eriu Remember - Lessons and teachings embedded in myths and legends of our sacred sites'*, November 2022

- *'Ancient Ancestors Calling! With words of wisdom and knowledge for today's world'*, - December 2022

- *Wake Up! This is it! The Great Apocalypse! - There is nothing hidden that will not be revealed'.* May 2023

- *'The Simulator. Are we living in a simulation? Are we trapped? If so, how do we escape?'*, July 2023

- *'The Soul Net! Does it exist? Are we a trawling ground for energy vampires and other-worldly parasites? How doe we avoid getting caught?'*, September 2023

- *'This is OUR STORY! - The story of Humanity! - As in the ancient Sumerian Clay Tablets! - And the Missing Link?'*, January 2024

- *'Through The Lens of the 3rd Eye. A new perspective! Vision beyond sight!'*, February 2024

- *'What's In A Name?- The Magdalene Institutions in 20th-Century Ireland '*, May 2024

And now this current *book*, - **'And The Walls Came Tumbling Down - The Rise and Demise of the Catholic Church in 20th-Century Ireland'.**

Podcasts for each of these 50 books can be viewed on Eileen's website and on her author page.

Eileen has also just recently re-published a series of 5 local history books under the title '**Finding Our Way Back**'. These were first published in the 1980s:

Book One: '**Strange Happenings**' - a 1988 collection of local ghost stories and local cures and charms, collected by the students of Saint Patrick's College Armagh.

Book Two: '**Tell Me More, Grandad!**' - a collection of school day memories collected from grandparents and great-grandparents in 1990.

Book Three: '**Gather In, Gather In**', - a collection of children's games and rhymes, 1942-1943, by the late Mr. Paddy Hamill, collected from the pupils in Lislea No 2 Primary School 1939 to 1947 when Mr. Hamill was Principal

Book Four: '**A Peep Into The Past: Armagh in Great-Granny's day**' - Earlier maps of Armagh, explaining how Armagh got its street names, together with photographs of streets and shop-fronts in the early 20th century. Also included is information on schools and education in Armagh in the 19th Century; newspaper articles of interest from 1848; traders in Armagh in 1863 and markets and fairs in Armagh, - of which there were many!

Book Five: "**The Poor Law And The Workhouse In Armagh 1838-1948**' - prepared when Eileen was on secondment in the Public Record Office of Northern Ireland, 1980-1981, under the scholarship scheme provided for teachers by the Department of Education. The resulting publication was used in local schools for coursework for examination purposes. Primary sources include the Armagh workhouse registers and minute books, which are all held in the Northern Ireland Public Record Office in Belfast; government commissions and reports; annual reports of the Poor Law Commission for Ireland 1847-1921, and photographs of the inside and outside of Armagh workhouse, now part of Tower Hill Hospital, taken in 1989 by the late Mary Donnelly (nee Finn), Saint Patrick's College, Armagh.

The recent series of FB weekly videos, **'Our Great Awakening',** together with the previous series **'The Nature of........'** with Eileen and Declan Quigley, Shamanic practitioner and teacher can also be viewed on Eileen's website and on YouTube, together with a series of healing meditations and Shamanic journeys.

Recent Full Moon Meditations with Declan Quigley, Jennifer Maddy and Brenda Murnaghan can be viewed on Eileen's YouTube channel, - access through website.

Also a series of videos on visits to various sacred sites around our country can be viewed on Eileen's FB page and YouTube channel.

Eileen has also recorded 6 guided meditation CDs with her brother, composer/pianist Pat McCourt:

- **'Celestial Healing'**
- **'Celestial Presence'**
- **'Cleansing, energising and balancing the Chakras'**
- **'Ethereal Spirit'** - Meditation on the **'I Am Presence'**
- **'Open the Door to Archangel Michael'**
- **'Healing with Archangel Raphael'**

Eileen's first DVD, **'Living the Magic'** features a live interview in which Eileen talks about matters Spiritual.

All publications are available from Amazon online and all publications and CDs are in Angel and Holistic centres around the country, as specified on website.

Please visit also the BLOG page on Eileen's website.

Website: www.celestialhealing8.co.uk

Author page: www.eileenmccourt.co.uk

YouTube channel:

https://www.youtube.com/channel/UChJPprUDnI9Eeu0IrRjGsqw

the city of Dublin and at homes around the country. Seven great ocean liners were berthed along the quays, with five more around Scotsmans Bay, all acting as floating hotels and each with capacity to accommodate up to 1,500 people on board.

The '*Blue Hussars'*, a ceremonial cavalry unit of the Irish Army formed to escort the President of Ireland on state occasions, formed a guard of honour for the visiting papal legate, Cardinal Lorenzo Lauri, representing Pope Pius XI.

And what a remarkable week for John Charles McQuaid, president of Blackrock College, as he rose to the occasion! The same John Charles McQuaid who was soon to become the most powerful Catholic Church authority in Ireland!

It was in the grounds of Blackrock College that McQuaid hosted a large garden party to welcome the papal legate, accompanied by Monsignor Domentico Tardini the Under Secretary of the Sacred Congregation for Extraordinary Ecclesiastical Affairs, Frances Spellman of the Secretariat of State, and Monsignor Calderan the Pontifical Master of Ceremonies. The highest of the high, the elite of the Vatican! The many hundreds of assembled bishops mingled with a huge gathering of distinguished guests, 23,000 in total, including the Governor General, along with Éamon de Valera and others of societal elite.

That's how big this event was! An extravagant showpiece on an international stage! A '*holy show',* literally! The flamboyance of the ecclesiastical gathering, their various scarlet, purple, white and black robes dazzling and shimmering in the brilliant sunshine! McQuaid entertaining the very highest from both the Vatican and from the Irish State, as well as from the American, Australian, British and European Church hierarchy.

The newly independent Irish State, now with a separate identity from England, and with a high profile as a catholic nation, as opposed to protestant England, its former oppressor, its former colonial master.

And the theme of this 31st International Eucharistic Congress? As noted by various media outlets, in keeping with all previous congresses reflecting their own individual characteristics, - in Chicago, it was the *'enthusiasm of the Americans'*, in Rome it had been *'the everlasting glory of the church'*, in Spain, *'the love of beauty and gallantry of the Spanish'*, - and now in Ireland it would be *'the Faith of the Irish'*, with special emphasis on *'The Propagation of the Sainted Eucharist by Irish Missionaries'*.

The final public mass of the congress was held at 1 pm on Sunday 26th June in Phoenix Park, attended by over one million people and celebrated by Michael Joseph Curley, Archbishop of Baltimore. A radio station was set up in Athlone to coincide with the Congress. Known for the occasion as Radio Athlone, this was to become in 1938, Radio Éireann and later RTÉ Radio. The ceremonies included a live radio broadcast by Pope Pius XI from the Vatican. Count John McCormack, the world famous Irish tenor, sang César Franck's *'Panis Angelicus'* at the mass. The same *'Panis Angelicus'* that has been performed by the star tenors Andrea Bocelli and Luciano Pavarotti. *'Panis Angelicus'*, which translates as *'Bread of Angels'* is a verse from the hymn *'Sacris solemniis'*, which was written by Saint Thomas Aquinas for the Feast of Corpus Christi in the 13th century. And what do the lyrics mean? Translated from the Latin, it reads:

'May the Bread of Angels / Become bread for mankind; / The Bread of Heaven puts / all foreshadowings to an end; / Oh, thing miraculous! / The body of the Lord will nourish / the poor, the poor, / the servile, and the humble.'

And the rendering of this same *'Panis Angelicus'* on this most auspicious of occasions most certainly symbolised the bonding of catholicism and nationalism in this new independent Irish State.

Approximately 25% of the population of Ireland attended the mass, and afterwards four processions left Phoenix Park to go to O'Connell Street, where some 500,000 people were gathered on O'Connell Bridge, for the concluding benediction given by the papal legate, Cardinal Lorenzo Lauri.

But not everyone in Ireland rejoiced! The rank and file of protestant Ulster, recently separated from the catholic independent Free State by partition, made their opposition known. However, despite their objections, the Congress was considered to be an overwhelming and incredible success.

A '*holy show*' indeed, if ever there was one!

And the legacy of the 1932 Eucharistic Congress? A strong, solidified bonding between Church and people, cemented now in the Catholic religion! That very same bond that the British had tried unsuccessfully for centuries to break. And the establishment of John Charles McQuaid, not just as headmaster, but as an organiser of extraordinary ability, an educationalist, a theologian, and a robust figure of the establishment. McQuaid's star was rising! He was on his way!

Let us fast forward now to 29th September - 1st October 1979. Another iconic date, another iconic event indeed, in the entire history of Irish Catholicism. This time the pope himself did come, - John Paul II. And the entire country was on the move! All roads leading to '*Il Papa*'! The entire country tuned into this papal visit! Everything geared towards this great Catholic Church event! All traffic, including public transport, banned from Dublin city centre, Dublin airport closed to all planes except that of Il Papa, and even a planned debate for that weekend on the '*Late Late Show*' on contraception cancelled out of deference and respect!

Pope John Paul II in Ireland! Over 2.5 million people gathered in various sites to join in the holy celebrations: Dublin's Phoenix Park; Killimer near Drogheda; Clonmacnoise; Galway; Knock; Limerick and Maynooth. In Phoenix Park, the Aer Lingus 747 '*St. Patrick*' carrying Pope John Paul to Ireland flew low over a crowd of 1,250,000 - one third of the population of the Irish Republic. At Clonmacnoise the crowd was 20,000, at Ballybrit racecourse in Galway 300,000. And at Knock, to mark the centenary of the reputed Marian apparitions, a crowd of 450,000 were gathered. At Maynooth, 1,000 seminarians joined a crowd of 450,000 to welcome Pope John Paul to Ireland, the first ever papal visit to our shores. The great, the good, the not-so-good and the mighty all out in force to welcome '*Il Papa*'! Nothing like this witnessed in Ireland since the visit of President John F. Kennedy back in 1963. And even the 1932 Congress dwarfed in comparison.

The Irish tenor John McCormack now dead, replaced by the equally famous Irish tenor Frank Patterson to sing at the mass in Phoenix Park; Archbishop John Charles McQuaid also dead, replaced by Monsignor John Magee as the chief organiser. And Tomás Ó Fiaich, recently appointed, in 1997, as Archbishop of Armagh following the death of Cardinal William Conway, and for whom this was the first major event in his episcopacy. And it was Ó Fiaich who was at the pope's side during the entire papal visit.

Huge numbers indeed! And those who could not get to a site, watched it on television. And all, as one newspaper reported, amid *'outpourings of joy and fervour'*, another describing it as unprecedented '*mass hysteria*', - and all because '*Il Papa*' was coming.

And we all assumed at the time that '*Il Papa*' was here in a special tribute to the country's Catholic fidelity. An acknowledgement of Ireland's adherence to the Catholic Church.

Holy Catholic Ireland! Sure were we not all elated? All basking in the pontifical approval of his Holiness! The man himself, '*Il Papa*' had come to visit **US**! And we cheered and roared and waved as if it was the expected '*Second Coming*'! Or maybe even '*Elvis the Pelvis*' back from the dead!

But nothing is ever as it seems! - Oh no!

They say that '*hindsight is a wonderful thing!*'. And they're right! Hindsight is indeed a wonderful thing! Meaning that the further away from an event or happening you go, the clearer it becomes in perspective. Just like if you stand up close to a wall and stare at just one brick. You see only that one brick. But take a few steps back, and you see the whole wall. A few more steps back and you see the whole building, a few more and you see the entire street, and so on. Or like the little grub or insect crawling along the ground. Totally immersed and submerged in its immediate surroundings, its vision severely limited by the blades of grass that are its sole environment. How different to the eagle! The eagle that soars above everything! The eagle that sees the whole picture! The eagle that has the complete view!

So with insightful hindsight, we can now put that iconic visit into its correct historical context.

We were not the only country to get such a visit in that same year. In 1979, Mexico and Poland also welcomed Pope John Paul. And in each, he spoke out about what his listeners might not have wanted to hear. In Mexico he spoke out about radical Latin American priests confusing Marxism with social justice. In Poland he spoke out about the country's closed borders and called upon his countrymen to press for more freedom.

And in Ireland? - In Ireland he spoke out about the need to renounce political violence, and the need to remain faithful to the Church and its teachings by rejecting the advances of materialism and secularism.

All straight references to the winds of change that were already beginning to blow across Ireland! Where the Irish Catholic hierarchy found themselves, for the first time ever, confronted by pastoral and leadership challenges with a quiet but growing faith crisis, a marked fall in religious vocations and the awful ongoing tragedy of the Northern Ireland Troubles, - and each of these was addressed by the pope while in Ireland.

Yes, it was indeed a momentous occasion. But was John Paul invited as a matter of urgency, or did he himself decide we needed a visit from the top brass? - And again, as a matter of urgency?

And why on earth would we possibly **need** a visit? What was so urgent?

The pope's words at Drogheda give us a clue!

'On my knees, I beg you to turn away from the path of violence and return to

the ways of peace.'

Those words were delivered just exactly one month after Louis Mountbatten was killed at Mullaghmore, County Sligo by the Provisional IRA, at the height of the Troubles in Ireland.

And at Ballybrit?

'Young people of Ireland, I love you!'

Emotional blackmail, many would say!

During his visit, John Paul made a point of engaging with young people, emphasising to them the importance of faith, hope, and love, encouraging them to actively participate in their communities and to contribute positively to society. And of course, young people are our future! The future of the Catholic Church depends on them! He was sounding a rallying call to the youth of Ireland!

At Ballybrit racecourse in Galway, he addressed families, emphasising the importance of family life, love, and commitment. And he warned the '*dear young people*' of Ireland against the challenges and the temptations of more freedom, the pleasures and attraction of materialism, and the dangers of losing the traditional moral values of previous generations:

'Like so many other young people in various parts of the world, you will be told that changes must be made, that you must have more freedom, that you should be different from your parents, and that the decisions about your lives depend on you, and you alone........The lure of pleasure, to be had whenever and wherever it can be found will be strong and it may be presented to you as part of progress towards greater autonomy and freedom from rules.

The desire to be free from external restraints may manifest itself very strongly in the sexual domain, since this is an area that is so closely tied to a human personality. The moral standards that the Church and society have held up to you for so long a time, will be presented as obsolete and a hindrance to the full development of your own personality......

Dear young people, do not close your eyes to the moral sickness that stalks your society today, and from which your youth alone will not protect you. How many young people have already warped their consciences and have substituted the true joy of life with drugs, sex, alcohol, vandalism and the empty pursuit of mere material possessions.'

In the Dominican Convent in Drogheda, he met with religious sisters, acknowledging their contributions to education, healthcare, and social services.

Throughout his visit, he consistently emphasised the need for peace, reconciliation, and unity in Ireland, - an Ireland experiencing political and sectarian tensions. Overall, his agenda focused on spiritual guidance, fostering unity, and encouraging positive social change. And an adherence to the Catholic Church! To the *'Faith of our Fathers'*.

Get the picture? We needed to be pulled back from the path along which we appeared to be straying! A path that was leading us away from the control of the Catholic Church! We were becoming morally sick! And the young people needed to be reined in! We all needed the noose to be tightened! The Rome connection to be re-enforced! *'Il Papa'* was here on a mission! And let us be very clear what that mission was! - To prop and bolster up the conservative Roman Catholic faith and doctrine! The signs were there, - the faith in the Catholic Church was fading, young people were falling away, and religious vocations were down. A younger, more vigorous pope had come to the rescue!

At Galway, two clerics were entertaining the waiting crowds, hyping them up, pumping up the adrenalin, whipping up mass hysteria, with an enthusiastic rendition of *'He's got the whole world in his hands'*, *'On the rivers of Babylon'*, *'Bind us together Lord!'* - the warm-up duo of the jovial, affable, singing Bishop Eamon Casey and alongside him, the equally jovial, affable, singing Father Michael Cleary. Cleary, who loved music and singing, and author of the book '*The Singing Priest*'. Cleary, who had put himself in the spotlight as an entertainer, with his own call-in radio show and TV interview programme. The charismatic Cleary, with his '*cool*' image, the '*hip, hop and happening*' cleric, the '*trendy*' priest, with a special appeal to young people. Cleary and Casey, with their popular '*people*' touch, - the link, the connecting bridge between the dull, inward-looking, aloof and remote Catholic hierarchy and the vibrant, out-reaching world of the new youth of Ireland.

So no two better men to be chosen to entertain the crowds at Galway, all waiting for the pope to arrive! Waiting for '*Il Papa*'. Many who had trekked through fields and camped overnight, arriving in the darkness to find their designated enclosure, to be in place in their allotted space in time for tomorrow morning's excitement. Bus loads arriving from every parish in the country! All obeying orders to turn out in full force!

Both men, of different generations, - Cleary the younger, - had been outspoken about the sacredness of marriage, the evils of sex outside of marriage, and against divorce and abortion. Cleary, later, in 1983 was prominent in the ranks of the Church, taking a strong stance against and promoting a '*no*' return on the abortion referendum, and again in 1995 on the divorce referendum.

But! Two clerics who were '*fathers*', not just in the ecclesiastical meaning of the word, but also biologically. But this was all for revelation in the future!

And the irony in all this? It must surely be that the very '*moral decline*' to which John Paul was referring, and those who would open the clerical proverbial can of worms were not out there in the sea of cheering faces in front of him, or sitting at home watching on television, but right there beside him on that podium! But who could possibly have known it?

And so it was that Pope John Paul II came to Ireland! To make sure that we remained faithful! To shepherd his straying flock back into the Catholic fold! To arrest the declining institutional influence of the Catholic Church! To reverse a quiet but growing faith crisis! To rally the youth to its cause! To bring about a cessation of violence in Northern Ireland! And to bolster us all up within the folds of the Catholic Church!

But those expectations were misplaced and misguided. Ireland in the late 1970s and early 1980s was an Ireland that was already breaking away from traditional values, an Ireland where a desire for material advancement, future progress, and individual moral freedom, as in the rest of the world, was replacing inherited blind faith and fidelity to a spiritual past, to an institution that had become outdated and outmoded. An institution rapidly becoming no longer fit for purpose!

In September 1983, just four years after Pope John Paul's visit, - and after much of the twentieth century where Ireland was unique among western countries in not permitting abortion, contraception, or divorce, - the abortion referendum in Ireland returned 67% in favour of legal abortion, 33% against.

In 1995, the divorce referendum in Ireland returned 50.78% for a change in the divorce laws and 49.72% against.

And in May 2015, Ireland voted in a countrywide referendum for gay marriage, becoming the only country in the world to pass such a law by a public vote.

The people of Ireland were speaking! Throwing off the shackles! *'Change'*, and not *'chains'* was becoming the operative word!

Clearly making the statement that adherence to Church teaching on social and moral matters, such as abortion, divorce, gay marriage and pre-marital sexual relations, which for decades had been the predominant concern of the hierarchy, had sharply declined. Despite the Church stronghold, the percentage of births outside marriage grew from 4 per cent in 1977 to 31.4 per cent in 2005; the divorce rate among Catholics in 2016 was 4.1 per cent, up from 3.6 per cent in 2011.

In 1979, when Pope John Paul came to Ireland, those winds of change had already begun to blow! The demise of the Catholic Church in Ireland had already set in! On the slow burner, yes, but already started! The closed Irish society was opening up!

And that was why Pope John Paul II came to Ireland in 1979. - To arrest the moral decline!

His visit came at a time when the zenith of the power of the Catholic Church in Ireland had already passed, the decline had already begun. That zenith had been 1932 and the Eucharistic Congress! We did not know it then, - but we know it now! Monsignor John Magee, from County Down, a rising star in the Vatican, known far and wide as private secretary to no less than three popes, and suspected by many of involvement in the mysterious death of one of them, - Pope John Paul I, who died on September 28th 1978, after just thirty-three days in the pontifical office. John Magee, now the key figure in the visit of the newly-elected John Paul II to Ireland, in charge of all the arrangements, and standing right there next to him throughout every event. But John Magee, like many other men of the holy cloth, was soon to become a fallen star! But again, all this was for revelation in the future.

And Pope John Paul's legacy in Ireland? In the immediate aftermath and short term, - a renewed atmosphere of piety, holiness and religiosity, a return to full churches and deep expressions of devotion and faith.

But long-term, and his greatest legacy? Hundreds of new-born baby boys named John Paul!

Let us fast forward again now to 25th/26th August 2018. Another papal visit. A different pope - this time Pope Francis. And a very different scenario! What was the reason this time? What had we done, or not done, over the last forty years to warrant another visit?

Much smaller crowds than last time! Estimated at nearly 85% less! People going to work as usual - just another day. Getting on with it! Where the previous papal visit in 1979 was remarkable for the huge numbers attending, this one was mostly remarkable for the huge numbers not attending. A general air of permeating indifference, even apathy! Despite RTE's attempts to boost the numbers on our television screens! Miriam O'Callaghan standing on a raised platform in D'Olier Street in Dublin city centre, interviewing a young teenage girl, and enthusing about the vast crowds that were turning out to greet Pope Francis! But the street behind her was empty! D'Olier Street was empty! And I don't mean there were just a few people! I mean the street was empty! And it was raining! Pathetic fallacy or what? And the television cameras in Phoenix Park! 500,000 expected there, with 700 police on duty for the papal mass! A big drop from the 1,250,000 on the previous visit! RTE cameras focusing solely on where small groups of people were gathered. Avoiding the empty spaces! And no wide panoramic views or high overhead shots this time.

What a difference from the 1979 visit! All testimony indeed to the growing decline of the power of the Catholic Church in Ireland!

This 2018 visit cost an estimated 35 million Euro! 22 million of that raised by the Catholic Church, the rest contributed by the Irish Government. Religious memorabilia on sale everywhere! Hundreds of clergy turned out in full flamboyant regalia! Another '*holy show*'! Another attempted spectacular Church display! Another attempted show of Church power!

But an Ireland now in shock from the string of clerical sexual abuse scandals emerging in free fall! And the Church hierarchy seen to be doing nothing about it, except moving those perpetrators on to different parishes! And an Ireland now in shock from the revelations about the Magdalene Institutions that had begun to pour out! A Catholic Church riddled with intrigue, scandal, secrecy, corruption, and cover-ups!

Both disgraced Bishop Eamon Casey and Father Michael Cleary now dead, Monsignor John Magee, not dead, but in disgrace for covering up clerical abuse.

This time, it was Archbishop Diarmuid Martin of Dublin, as President of the

World Meeting of Families 2018, who was in charge of arrangements:

'We eagerly await the visit of Pope Francis, which no doubt will be an occasion of spiritual renewal for our laity, religious and clergy as well as a strengthening of Christian family life.'

But who exactly was the *'we'* being referred to here? On whose behalf was the Catholic Church speaking?

And the Catholic Bishops' Conference weighed in:

'We are deeply honoured that Pope Francis will come to our country to participate in this universal church celebration of faith and joy, as well as of the contemporary challenges which face families.

With great anticipation we also look forward to hearing the apostolic guidance of His Holiness during his stay with us.'

A visit that was not without controversy! This was 2018, and Ireland had moved on! Moved on from the total suffocating grip of the Catholic Church on all aspects of Irish life! And in 2018, people were not afraid to openly protest! Protesting mostly about how clerical sexual abuse had all been covered up! And the scandals coming out about the Catholic-Church-run Magdalene institutions!

And the entertainment this time? It was *'Riverdance'* that got the loudest cheer, *'Riverdance'* that got feet jigging, *'Riverdance'* that had premiered on the world stage at the 1994 Eurovision Song Contest. And Daniel O'Donnell and his wife Majella, married since 2002, Majella having secured a legal divorce through the Catholic Church!

Yes, Ireland had moved on! Divorce, gay marriage, abortion, abuse in the Catholic run Magdalene homes, in orphanages, in residential homes, in industrial training schools and in other institutions, - all out now in the open! And protestors showing their disapproval of such a visit from a pope who had still done nothing about all the clerical sex scandals and constant cover-ups!

So! 1979 and 2018. What had happened in the intervening almost 40 years to bring about such a remarkable and irreversible change? The irreversible decline of the power of the Catholic Church in Ireland! That's what happened!

At the zenith of its power in 1932, but by the 1960s, change was already happening, and by the dawn of the present 21st century, the decline of the power of the Catholic Church in Ireland had rapidly advanced. A paradox indeed if ever there was one! - A rapidly advancing decline!

In 1950, Archbishop John Charles McQuaid had ordained a record 67 students to the priesthood at Maynooth. 1950 was the *'high-water mark of an era when every family aspired to produce a priest or a nun.'* (*'John Charles McQuaid - Catholic Ruler of Ireland'*, John Cooney, page 235)

In 1965, there were 400 seminarians but by 2023 the number was just 10. A rapidly advancing decline!

The Catholic Church that had the power, under McQuaid, to dictate and write significant parts of the 1937 Irish Constitution; the power of that same Catholic Church, under McQuaid, to bring down a government, or great political leaders, as did Cardinal Cullen with Charles Stuart Parnell in the 19th century and now McQuaid with Dr. Noel Browne in the 20th century; the power of that same Catholic Church, under McQuaid, to dictate, determine and control government policies such as education, health and social welfare! That power was now no more. Gone, gone for good!

And the walls came tumbling down! The huge edifice that had been the Catholic Church in Ireland in the mid 20th century was collapsing on all sides! A tumbling deck of cards! A falling set of dominoes!

Since 1990, the office of President of Ireland has been held by two females, - Mary Robinson and Mary McAleese; the office of Taoiseach - Prime Minister - has been held by an openly gay man; women have moved into all areas of public life; divorce, gay marriage and legal abortion are now part of the Irish scene. Churches that were once full are now almost empty. Mass attendance has fallen dramatically! And who actually goes to Confession any more?

The rise and demise of the Catholic Church in Ireland! How did that institution come to have so much power and suffocating, paralysing control over every aspect of people's lives in the late 19th and early to mid 20th century? Like a great creeping octopus, spreading its tentacles into every corner of every Irish home, even into the bedroom! And how did it lose that power?

That is what this book is investigating!

So let's get started!

xxvi

Chapter 1:

The institutional nature of the Catholic Church

In order to understand how the Catholic Church ever came to have so much power in Ireland, it is necessary to understand its innate structure and organisation. Because by that very same innate structure and organisation, by its very nature, and like every other denominational church, the Catholic Church is an institution. A money-making institution, just like any government in any part of our world.

And like all institutions, the Catholic Church is founded on the structure of the pyramid. A patriarchal, vast bureaucratic institution, with a huge organisational network that controls most social structures.

The pyramid! - A mega-structure! That most powerful of sacred symbols! Spiritually, the pyramid symbolises the earth, power, strength, enhancement and empowerment. And of course, like absolutely everything else, it also has a negative polarity. A negative polarity, where those working in that negative polarity are abusing and misusing the power of the pyramid for their own devious ends, - for control and manipulation, trapping the laity in a pyramidal structure which is not for their highest good.

And why the pyramid? - Because the pyramid is structured in such a way that power lies in the hands of the very few, the very few at the top who only themselves know exactly what is going on. All the others know little or nothing of the reality! They are simply pawns in a game which mostly they do not even know is being played! All shrouded in secrecy!

The manufacturing of the first atomic bomb in America exemplifies it all! The *'little man'* at the bottom putting in a screw or a bolt here or there had absolutely no idea what the finished product was going to be, or for what purpose it was going to be used. Not even the vice-president of America knew about it!

And in the Catholic Church we see the pyramidal structure. The pyramidal structure that enables those at the very top to hold onto power and control. The pope at the summit, in all his pontifical splendour and wealth, ensconced in his own self-declared holy, sacred and unquestionable *'infallibility'*, within the secure walls of the Vatican, the smallest independent sovereign nation in the world, with its own government and administrative systems, its own banking system, its own law courts and legal systems, known as Canon Law, all accountable only to the Vatican, - and where all the decisions are made with regard to Church dogma, teachings and beliefs. Untouchable! Next to the pope, we have the cardinals, - in all their scarlet-robed medieval Cardinal Wolsey-like flamboyance and ostentatiousness, then the archbishops and bishops, aloof and remote in their palatial mansions, with their chauffeur-driven cars, secretaries, housekeepers, and various attendants, then the parish priest and the various religious orders, and finally the curate in his local parish. The minions at the bottom who take orders from those above them, obeying without question. The minions at the bottom who are in direct contact with the masses. Delivering, through their Sunday sermons at mass, the messages from those at the top, delivering to a captive audience, mostly only there under duress, under threat of excommunication or eternal damnation!

And it is through this water-tight pyramidal structure, this highly developed bureaucratic apparatus, this hierarchal system of command from the pope down, that a rigorous code of discipline, order and strict adherence to Rome could and was implemented. A vast organisation that was developed in rural Ireland in the 19th century, an extension of bureaucratic rule from Rome, all under Cardinal Paul Cullen! Cardinal Paul Cullen who reshaped the rather raggedy, haphazard Catholic Church in Ireland along *'Roman'* Catholic lines. And in the twentieth century, as we shall see later, Archbishop John Charles

And the Walls Came Tumbling Down!

McQuaid! An organisation that totally controlled education, health and social welfare! And control of these organisations was absolutely vital to the Catholic Church maintaining its grip on the Irish nation. Denominational education in particular! Moulding the youth into the ethos of the Catholic Church! The youth being the adults of tomorrow!

The hierarchal structure where everyone, everyone in the *'club'*, and that is what it is, a club, - bishops, priests, nuns, religious orders, - all had a particular place and knew what their role was within the club. An organisation that seeped into every aspect of people's lives, where their daily life was spent under the supervision of one or other of Catholic Church infra-structure representatives! Home, school, hospital, church-going with weekly and daily mass, devotions, confessions, the sacraments, the home with the nightly rosary and adherence to fast days and prayers, the year based around Church festivals and holy days, - this was how the Catholic Church controlled people's lives, and how they kept this control! It was always there! Hovering over every aspect of daily life!

This hierarchically-structured power mechanism has regulated and controlled the laity simply through its very organisational strength. Enabling the Catholic Church to take control of moral discipline and practice in just the same way as the pyramidal structure of any government or state enables control in political matters. And just as in the political pyramid, so too, in the Church pyramid, we have the constant jockeying, jostling and vying for position. Every move made with a particular personal agenda in mind - to reach the top. To attain that absolute power!

The Catholic Church pyramid is a system into which one is usually born, and in which one is usually retained by the promise of eternal life for life-long membership, or the threat of eternal damnation for a lapsing of that same membership. From the cradle to the grave - and all in between! And of course not forgetting personal career promotion and societal upward mobility if one stays obediently within the ranks!

A holy, sacred club! Its upper members distinguished by their clerical dressage and ceremonial attire, - *'the gear'* , as one particular archbishop termed it, by their *'reputed'* vows of poverty, chastity and obedience, and by the extreme reverence in which they are held by the laity, untouchable and unquestionable on their elevated holy pedestals.

Wheels within wheels! Pyramids within pyramids! Like a set of Russian dolls! All nestled and encapsulated within one another! All holding each other up! And within the Church pyramid, we have an education pyramid, a health care pyramid, a social welfare pyramid, etc. etc. etc. -Tentacles everywhere!

Upward mobility only possible if one adheres strictly to the rules and is committed to preserving the system. A system that is designed to preserve itself at all costs! An unassailable organisational structure, where everyone has their place in the hierarchy, and it works as long as everyone obeys the old adage *'keep the rule, and the rule will keep you'*. Presidents and leaders are *'selected,'* not *'elected'*, and it is the same in the Church. The pope is *'selected'*, chosen from amongst his cronies, as are the cardinals and bishops. And all in secret! Nothing democratic about any of it! All autocracy! And all veiled in secrecy! All veiled in mystery! The laity or the lower rank-and-file curates have no say or vote in any of this. Yes, - popes, cardinals and bishops are *'selected'*, not elected. Selected by those at the very top of the pyramid! Selected because they will keep the system intact!

Bishops, directly below the cardinals in the pecking order of the pyramidal structure, appoint parish priests, who in turn oversee the local curates in their respective parishes. Bishops are also responsible for overseeing the operations of religious orders, but no bishop can censure a member of any religious order as easily as he can censure a diocesan priest - that is for the superior of each religious order. Hence, Fr. Brendan Smyth, the notorious paedophile, being a member of the Norbertine order, could only be censored by his own superior. And so it was that Smyth could take sanctuary in his monastery at Holy Faith Abbey in Ballyjamesduff, County Cavan. And all his superior did was move him on to pastures new, on to fresh hunting grounds!

And much further down the pyramid, the task of the diocesan priests is to preach, catechise and administer the sacraments. They are responsible for the spiritual welfare of their parishioners, being the only Catholic Church personnel in direct contact with the laity, but this often extends to their social welfare as well! Self-appointed caretakers! Watchdogs, more like! A sort of Big Brother figure! Watching, listening, in order to maintain power and control! Knowing what was going on in the schools, in the halls and in the homes, having detailed knowledge of the daily behaviour of his parishioners, - this was all vital for the priest to be able to assert his authority! And his two main means of securing that knowledge? Visits to the homes and through the confessional! That was where he heard everything! At the zenith of Catholic Church power in Ireland, the priest acted not just as a spiritual and moral adviser, but also as a political, social and economic authority. The priest was present on every committee, at every social event, every community activity. The priest was there to bless a new home, a new car, to advise on health and financial matters, marriage problems and the education of the children. To bury the dead, to baptise new infants, to perform the marriage ceremony into which his own input was great. The priest was everywhere!

And his authority and power was so great that he could denounce anyone he so wished, and so destroy one's social prestige! His power and authority so great that he was deferred to on all occasions, and could dictate on contraception, divorce and other matters of marriage intimacy. And he himself not even married!

A career in the Church! Historically, the first-born son inherited the estate; the second-born son joined the army, paying of course for his promotion, and the third-born son joined the Church! Again, paying for his position and upward mobility! Just think of the Borgias in medieval times! Pomp, splendour, ceremony! Wealth beyond our imagination! Simony, corruption, political and ecclesiastical intrigue, plotting, scheming and conniving - it was all there! All in the highest ecclesiastical office of the Papal Episcopacy!

The power of the pope at the top of this vast edifice! Bolstered up by his cardinals, archbishops and bishops. And we need to understand this pyramidal system and structure of power and control if we are ever going to get our heads around how this same Catholic Church came to have so much power and control in Ireland, how such a dictatorial, hierarchal, patriarchal Catholic Church come to be synonymous with Ireland? How *'Irish'* and *'Catholic'* became synonymous. How political parties bowed down to the Church, fawning and deferring, knowing that their political survival depended on the backing of the Church! The Catholic Church that had in their firm grasp the power of the public ballot box!

The organisation of the Catholic Church in Ireland is based on the division of the country into 26 dioceses, which are subdivided into parishes, each with a parish priest at the head. And as we have seen, in this tiered, hierarchal system, the parish priest controls the other priests in his parish. He himself is under the control of a bishop, who in turn is under the control of a cardinal. The cardinal is at the top in each country, immediately below the pope in Rome. So, under the hierarchal system of the Catholic Church, bishops are accountable to Rome, priests are accountable to their bishops, and the laity is accountable to their priests. A typical pyramidal structure!

Traditionally, bishops remain aloof from the laity. This is often explained by the fact that bishops are appointed for their academic ability, not from amongst the ranks of the curates, but from senior positions in Maynooth Catholic Seminary, from some other prestigious educational establishment, or from some notable service in Rome, and so have had no experience in personal contact with the laity or attending to the needs of the flock. And so the often-made claim that bishops are out of touch with the ordinary people can be easily explained! But their place in the pyramidal structure does not require bishops to have contact with the ordinary people! That's the whole point in the pyramid! It's all about power and control!

And the Walls Came Tumbling Down!

How Ireland became a theocracy! A theocratic state being defined as one that is governed by immediate divine guidance or by officials who are regarded as divinely guided. In other words, a priestly or religious body wielding both political and civil power. And that is what Ireland had become! A theocracy!

And it was the pyramidal system that enabled that! The pyramidal structure that placed education, health and social welfare all within the hands of the Catholic Church clergy! Every aspect of life in their control! The tentacles of the octopus!

And the reward for adhering to all of this? The reward for sustaining the system? The reward for being willing to stay within the boundaries set by those at the top of the pyramid?

A job! A career! Promotion! Is it not indeed remarkable how so many Blackrock College pupils, for example, rose to high positions in various walks of life? Blackrock College, where McQuaid ruled supreme! Blackrock College where McQuaid laid the foundations for his own upward move! Blackrock College, established by McQuaid as the very centre of all ecclesiastical events, every *'holy show'* in Ireland! To coin a phrase, the old cliche, - *'Jobs for the boys'*!

According to Wikipedia, past pupils of Blackrock College include early Irish Free State ministers such as Art O'Connor, Secretary for Agriculture 1921-1922; Éamon de Valera, six times Taoiseach and the 3rd President of Ireland who both studied and later taught in Blackrock College; Alfred O'Rahilly 1884-1969, a noted academic, President of University College Cork and a TD for Cork City: James McNeill, an Irish politician and diplomat, who served as the first High Commissioner to London and second Governor-General of the Irish Free State from 1927 to 1932.

Modern politicians include Ruairi Quinn, T.D., an Irish former Labour Party politician who served as Minister for Education and Skills from 2011 to 2014, Leader of the Labour Party from 1997 to 2002, Deputy Leader of the Labour

Party from 1989 to 1997, Minister for Finance from 1994 to 1997, Minister for Enterprise and Employment from 1993 to 1994, Minister for the Public Service from 1986 to 1987, Minister for Labour from 1983 to 1986, and Minister of State for Urban Affairs and Housing from 1982 to 1983. He served as a TD for the Dublin South-East constituency from 1977 to 1981 and 1982 to 2016. He was a Senator from 1976 to 1977, after being nominated by the Taoiseach and again from 1981 to 1982 for the Industrial and Commercial Panel; Barry Andrews, a teacher, served as TD for Dún Laoghaire from 2002 until 2011. He was the Minister for Children from 2008 until 2011; Rory O'Hanlon TD for Cavan–Monaghan 1977 until 2011 who served in a range of cabinet positions and as Ceann Comhairle of Dáil Éireann; Niall Ó Brolcháin Mayor of Galway from 2006 to 2007, who also served as a county councillor and senator; David P. Doyle, Ambassador, St. Kitts and Nevis to UNESCO.

And in legal circles: Ronan Keane, Former Chief Justice of the Supreme Court of Ireland; Dermot Gleeson, Former Attorney General, Chairman of AIB; Michael Moriarty, John Quirke and David Barniville, all High Court Judges; Seamus Egan, former Justice of the Supreme Court of Ireland; Vivion de Valera, T.D. son of Éamon de Valera; Rossa Fanning, Attorney General.

Then we have those who made it from Blackrock College into the highest ranks of the Catholic hierarchy! John Charles McQuaid himself, President of Blackrock College 1931-1939, later to become Catholic Archbishop of Dublin and Primate of Ireland between December 1940 and January 1972; Cardinal John D'Alton; Donal Murray, Bishop of Limerick; Emil August Allgeyer C.S.Sp., French born priest, first ordination in Blackrock in 1900, served in Trinidad and as a Bishop in Africa; Eugene Joseph Butler C.S.Sp., Bishop of Zanzibar, and Bishop of Mombasa; Robert Ellison B.Sc., S.T.L., C.S.Sp., Bishop of Banjul, Gambia; John Gerald Neville DD, C.S.Sp. 1858–1943, Bishop of Zanzibar, and Kenya, ordained a bishop in Blackrock in 1913; Ambrose Kelly C.S.Sp., Bishop of Freetown and Bo, Sierre Leon; Daniel Liston BA, BCL, DD, C.S.Sp., Bishop of Port Louis in Mauritius 1947–1968; John Joseph McCarthy C.S.Sp., Bishop of Nairobi, Kenya; Michael Joseph Moloney C.B.E., C.S.Sp., 1912–1991, Bishop of

Banjul, Gambia; John Joseph O'Gorman, C.S.Sp., first Bishop from the Irish Holy Ghost Fathers, first Bishop of Sierra Leone; John C. O'Riordan, C.S.Sp., Bishop of the Roman Catholic Diocese of Kenema in Sierra Leone; Joseph Brendan Whelan, BA, S.T.L, C.S.Sp. 1909–1990, served as Bishop of Owerri in Nigeria.

And others who made it to the top of their profession? -

Fr. Michael Doheny who was a founding member of Concern; Frank Duff, founder of the Legion of Mary; Bob Geldof, singer, songwriter, author, Live-Aid organiser and political activist; Ryan Tubridy, Irish broadcaster, presenter of live shows on radio and television in Ireland; Tim Pat Coogan, Irish writer, broadcaster and newspaper columnist, best-known for such books as *'The IRA', 'Ireland Since the Rising', 'On the Blanket',* and biographies of Michael Collins and Éamon de Valera, attended Blackrock College in the late 1940s; designer Paul Costelloe; the eminent writer Brian O' Nolan, author of *'At Swim-Two-Birds',* 1939 and *'The Third Policeman',* 1967, under the pen name Flann O'Brien and also satirical columns in The Irish Times under the pseudonym Myles na gCopaleen; Pádraic Ó Conaire 1882-1928, writer and journalist who wrote in Irish, particularly about Irish emigrants in the UK; Liam O'Flaherty 1896-1984, novelist and short story writer, known for *'The Informer';* Paddy Murray, journalist, who served as Editor of the Sunday Tribune from 2002 to 2005.

And as a further reward, Blackrock College has immortalised and continues to pay homage to its historical founders and other influential figures through its six student house names: De Valera, Duff, Ebenrecht, Leman, McQuaid and Shanahan.

The pyramidal system that gives absolute power to those few or that one person at the top! Power corrupts. And absolute power? Absolute power corrupts absolutely!

And so it is that we are continuing to see powerful establishments and institutions tumble down all around us!

Today the victor, tomorrow the vanquished! Today the victor, tomorrow the victim. All great civilisations rise and fall, as history has shown. As do institutions! And the Catholic Church is just that, - an institution!

But one of the most powerful and most wealthy institutions in the world!

Chapter 2:

All God's Men!

Irish and Catholic synonymous - how did that happen?

Holy Catholic Ireland! The 1932 Eucharistic Congress held in Ireland! What an honour! That auspicious date and that historic congress marked the zenith of the power of the Catholic Church in Ireland. No one could have foreseen that by 1979 when Pope John Paul II came to visit, that power was already somewhat in decline. That was why he came! We just did not know it at the time! We thought his visit was surely an acknowledgement of Ireland as a staunch Catholic country, loyal to Rome and to the Catholic Church! And how we basked in that papal approval! *'Irish'* and *'Catholic'* had indeed become synonymous.

But by 2018, when Pope Francis came to visit, the decline of the power of the Catholic Church in Ireland was irreversibly well under way. To understand how this happened, how the terms *'Irish'* and *'Catholic'* were no longer synonymous, we need to retrace our steps back to 432 AD and the *'reputed'* arrival of Saint Patrick in Ireland. Saint Patrick, - he who managed to convert, almost overnight, pagan Ireland! He who managed to get rid of all those non-existent *'snakes'*! Saint Patrick - symbolic of the coming of Christianity to Ireland. And the *'snakes'*? - Symbolic of the pagans! The triumph of Christianity over paganism! Whether you believe in the story or not, Christianity, the Roman Christian Church, founded by the Romans in the fourth century, had arrived in Ireland.

The early Roman Christian Church in Ireland, as was the set-up elsewhere, had its bishops and priests. But the early Irish Christian Church quickly became monastic, with groups of priests coming together all over the country in primitive monastic settlements, and within a brief period of time, the monasteries were the organisational centres of the Church in Ireland. The monasteries became thriving, wealthy centres of culture and religion, and also the power-houses from which there developed a remarkable missionary forward movement, with Irish monks leaving Ireland to establish monasteries in other countries, and becoming enormously influential on religion and culture throughout the continent of Europe.

Around 800 AD, the golden age of the Irish Christian Church was declining with the invasions and raidings of the Vikings and the Danes. And why did they come? They came to plunder! Attracted by the wealth of the monastic establishments!

Church reform began again in the twelfth century, and in 1169 the Cambro-Norman invasion brought the first Norman settlers from Wales, many of whom intermarried with the native Irish and became *'more Irish than the Irish themselves'*. Politics and religious divisions became intertwined very quickly.

The 16th century Protestant Reformation in England, separating England from the Church of Rome, when Henry VIII was determined to divorce Catherine of Aragon, increased tension and division between Ireland and England, as Ireland remained Catholic. Increasingly viewed now as a serious threat to the safety of England, a back door for England's Catholic enemies in Europe, Ireland was subjected to persecution and a series of plantations, particularly successful in Ulster in 1606.

The Penal Laws passed against the Catholics in the 18th century deprived them of any ownership of land, education or political rights and kept them locked in secure boundaries. They were a threat to the new Protestant Ascendancy class. However, during this time, over thirty Irish colleges were established on the European mainland and hence many Irish still managed to receive an education for the priesthood.

The Catholic Stuart claim to the throne of England, supported by the Catholic Irish, ended in a series of defeats, removing the threat and so the English government began to relax the Penal Laws and grant some concessions to the Irish Catholics.

In 1829, Daniel O'Connell secured Catholic Emancipation, and so began the restoration of the Catholic Church in Ireland. A huge milestone was the foundation of Maynooth College in County Kildare in 1795, for the education of priests.

And so it was that the Catholic Church began its restoration and domination of Irish society. Helped of course by the fact that most people saw Protestant England as the enemy and so the Irish were automatically defiantly *'Catholic'*. After the 1800 Act of Union, uniting Ireland with England, resistance to English rule took the form of the growth of agrarian secret societies, with the Young Irelanders and the Fenians all coming to be identified with this Catholic Ireland, - all in opposition to Protestant England. Politics and religion continuing to be intertwined.

Then came Independence, 1922. Many would say it was a story of *'Brits out! Catholic Church in!'*

And with independence, the Irish Catholic Church became highly organised. That was the key! Organisation! In fact, no institution was more significant in shaping the nature of Irish society after independence in 1922 than the Catholic Church, the *'institutional church'*, already described in the previous chapter. Meaning the dictatorial leadership of its bishops and archbishops, in the pyramidal hierarchal structure, who by the 1930s steered the Catholic Church to the height of its power in Ireland. The Catholic Church, Ireland's most powerful institution, with control over education, health and social services, enjoyed unprecedented power and influence right up until the 1960s, playing a central role in the process of state-building after political independence in 1922.

Nothing ever happens by chance, luck or coincidence! Simply because there is no such thing! Every happening is bound in with the great cosmic law, the great spiritual principle of '**cause and effect**'! All in an ongoing spiral movement. Even the fall of the dice is subject to this great cosmic law! Antecedent, present and consequent! Three words that cannot be separated!

So who were the main movers, makers and shakers who built up the power of the Catholic Church in the late 19th century and early-to-mid 20th century Ireland? The main movers, makers and shakers who made Irish and Catholic synonymous? The main movers, makers and shakers who were the **cause** of the rise of the power of the Catholic Church in Ireland?

Two members in particular of the Catholic Church hierarchy stand out. Two power-hungry men, in two different centuries, who fully understood the power they had in the pyramidal Church system, and who knew how to use it! Two men who gave their name to the era in which they lived! Just as history refers to the '*Victorian Age*' for example, or the '*Elizabethan Age*', so too, in the history of Irish Catholicism and indeed of the Irish State, we refer to the '*Cullen Era*' and the '*McQuaid Era',* sometimes even combining them both into the one, - '*Cullen/McQuaid Era'.*

Cardinal Paul Cullen, the first Irish Cardinal, 1849-1878, and John Charles McQuaid, Archbishop of Dublin and Primate of Ireland 1940-1972. Paul Cullen who, more than any other, fashioned a particular brand of Catholic life in Ireland, uniquely Irish-style, after the Church emerged from the dark years of the Penal Laws! Paul Cullen, over twenty years working at the Vatican, and Head of the Irish College in Rome, and hence amongst the top in the Church pyramid! Well equipped for heading the Catholic Church in Ireland!

And John Charles McQuaid, who embodied Cullen's uniquely grafted Irish-style Catholicism and brought it to its zenith. A period often referred to as '*Post-Emancipation Catholicism'.* John Charles McQuaid whose reign lasted even longer than Cullen's, - McQuaid for 32 years, Cullen for 29.

Paul Cullen first.

And the Walls Came Tumbling Down!

Cardinal Paul Cullen was the towering, dominant figure of modern Irish Catholicism and arguably also the most important political figure in modern Irish history between the death of Daniel O'Connell and the rise of Charles Stewart Parnell. Politics and religion continuing to be intertwined!

Paul Cullen! Ireland's first cardinal! And how did Paul Cullen achieve that coveted *'Red Hat'*? The first *'Red Hat'* for Ireland! - By *'Romanising'* the Catholic Church in Ireland! Obedience to Rome! The one consistent and common factor in all of his work was obedience to Rome! Bringing all and sundry under the banner of *'Roman'* Catholicism. And with this aim in mind, he played a crucial role in defining Papal *'infallibility'* at the First Vatican Council in 1870. That was his ticket, his brownie point, his claim for the *'Red Hat'*.

In August 1850, within a year of his appointment, Cullen, as Apostolic Delegate to Ireland and Archbishop of Armagh, assembled the first gathering of Catholic Church leaders in Ireland since that of the 1642 Confederation of Kilkenny. The Synod of Thurles, held in St. Patrick's College, Thurles in County Tipperary was Cullen's attempt to standardise the administration, religious practices, teaching and discipline of the Catholic Church in Ireland. Practices in the Church in Ireland had evolved differently from practices in continental Europe due to state suppression of the Church in Ireland from about 1640 until Catholic Emancipation in 1829. In advance of the synod, Cullen had been in Rome where he was appointed as Apostolic Delegate which in effect give him direct papal authority over the Catholic Church in Ireland.

Cullen's Synod of Thurles was an elaborate occasion, by any standards, never minding the date 1850, just after the Famine! The *'Illustrated London News'* gave it great coverage, describing a long procession of 300 religious men dressed in full splendid, flamboyant regalia, altar boys carrying their trains, and winding their way through the gates of St. Patrick's College Thurles, all to the accompanying sound of tolling church bells and Gregorian chanting. The newspaper describes:

'A gorgeous....array of coped and mitred bishops, their vestments of the richest

and costliest materials - velvet, brocade, or cloth of gold, and their mitres gleaming with jewels.' ('*The Best Catholics in the World*', Derek Scally, page 204)

And all this splendour while people, still ravaged by hunger and disease, in the aftermath of the Famine, knelt in the dirt, totally in awe of the holy spectacle processing right there in front of them.

And as Derek Scally writes:

'This is the symbolic starting point of modern Irish Catholicism: a people in rags, soiled capes and tattered bonnets, survivors of hunger, fever, eviction and violence, literally on their knees, as well-fed clerics glide by like demi-gods with a rustle of silk, the glisten of gold.' ('*The Best Catholics in the World*', Derek Scally, page 205)

The Synod of Thurles stamped Cullen's mark on Catholicism in Ireland. Rigid structures, high moral standards, elaborate ceremonies and rituals, with newly-built extravagant churches, absolute obedience and subservience to Rome, all now served to rebrand the Catholic Church in Ireland.

Cullen's pastoral vision extended far and wide, covering healthcare, education, church-building and a multitude of new institutions. He was particularly intent on promoting Roman Catholic religious education in Ireland, - but education '*Cullen-style*'! Education on a discriminatory basis! From the first days of his episcopate he had planned for a Roman Catholic university for Ireland, to equal the Protestant Trinity College. But at the same time, however, he sought religious and class segregation in the education system, insisting on the need for a limited curriculum for poorer Catholics as, in his own words, '*Too high an education will make the poor oftentimes discontented and will unsuit them for following the plough or for using the spade . . . The rich must have schools for themselves and learn many things not necessary for persons in a different state of life'.*

And the Walls Came Tumbling Down!

An uneducated peasant class! Illiterate! And hence easily controllable! Only the priests educated, and therefore looked up to and revered because of their education! They were the ones with the knowledge! They were the ones who knew!

Cullen it was who transformed Ireland into his vision for Rome! Into an enthusiastic branch of Catholicism! Into a bastion of Roman orthodoxy! Into a conservative and narrow-minded Ireland obsessed with denying sexuality and maintaining virginal purity! An Ireland where his priests were invested by him with unchallengeable and unquestionable authority! Looked up to and revered by not just the Irish people, but also by the civil and state authorities!

Cullen it was who forced upon the Irish people what he termed a *'devotional revolution'*. Meaning the introduction and implementation of devotional exercises such as the rosary, Marian devotion, devotion to the Sacred Heart, missions, retreats, perpetual adoration, novenas, vespers, the Angelus, and the use of devotional paraphernalia and aids such as mass missals, statues, holy water, holy pictures, miraculous medals, scapulars.

Cullen it was who instilled into Irish minds the supreme authority and infallibility of the leaders of the Catholic Church, and the elevation of priests in society, invested by Cullen with unchallengeable authority, to whom all must render obedience, and to whom all must defer and bow down.

Cullen it was who changed the Irish Catholic Church with his set of Rome-inspired decrees in 1850 which directed it away from Celtic traditions and towards Victorian prudishness.

And why was Cullen so devoted to the Virgin Mary? Why was he so insistent on establishing Marian devotion? On glorifying Mother Mary? - Simply because Mary, as a virgin, was pure, as she had not defiled her body by having sex! She was the epitome of womanhood! Virginity the preferred state for women! The Virgin Mary who gave birth to Jesus without having sex! A remarkable achievement indeed, by any standards!

And the principle of **'Cause and Effect'** already mentioned?

From where did all this come? All this abhorrence of the natural sexual act? All this associating the natural sexual act with human depravity? All this defamation of the feminine? In other words, what made Cullen to be as he became? What was the **cause**?

All this came from *'Jansenism'*, a Church belief associated with Cullen's reign.

'Jansenism', named after Dutch-born Cornelius Jansen who died in 1638, was an extreme form of doctrine based on a culture of shame and guilt, preaching as it did that original sin was caused by sexual depravity, and the body needed to be cleansed and purified of all impious thoughts and acts. And salvation could only be achieved through punishment, penance and suffering. Jansenism was strong in the Irish colleges throughout Europe and especially in France. It followed the preachings of St. Augustine, Bishop of Hippo Regius 354-430, on disgust of the human body, and his disgust of all things pertaining to women. In true early-Roman-Christian-Church-father style!

And what did Saint Augustine, Bishop of Hippo Regius 354-430, have to say about women? -

'Woman does not possess the image of God in herself but only when taken together with the male who is her head, so that the whole substance is one image.'

'What is the difference whether it is in a wife or a mother, it is still Eve the temptress that we must beware of in any woman. . . I fail to see what use woman can be to man, if one excludes the function of bearing children.'

'Woman is a misbegotten man and has a faulty and defective nature in comparison to his. Therefore she is unsure in herself. What she cannot get, she seeks to obtain through lying and diabolical deceptions.'

And after the repeal of the Penal Laws, in the period often referred to by historians as *'post-Emancipation Catholicism'*, and in the aftermath of the Famine, it was the doctrines associated with Jansenism, based on the teachings of St. Augustine, that the priests now returning from the Irish colleges in Europe brought back with them into Ireland.

And it was these same doctrines associated with Jansenism that Cullen now espoused, and ordered his priests to propagate! The doctrines of Jansenism that proclaimed purity of the mind, abhorrence and disgust of the body, man's unworthiness as a result of original sin, - original sin being the consequence of sexual depravity, and the need to cleanse the body and mind of all impious thoughts and acts. And all of this became ingrained into Cullen's own unique form of Catholicism! Catholicism Irish-style!

And there was another factor! - *'Ultramontanism'*.

'Ultramontanism' was a clerical-political belief within the Catholic Church that placed strong emphasis on the prerogatives and powers of the pope. The pope at the very top of the Catholic Church pyramid! He who must be obeyed! He who makes the rules! He who is *'infallible'*! Ultramontane Catholics emphasised the authority of the pope over temporal affairs of civil governments as well as the spiritual affairs of the Church. The term descends from the Middle Ages, when a non-Italian pope was said to be *'papa ultramontano'* – a pope from beyond the mountains, meaning from beyond the Alps. Foreign students at medieval Italian universities also were referred to as *'ultramontani'*.

So, slot Ultramontanism and Jansenism together, and what do we get? - We get Cardinal Paul Cullen! Ireland's first cardinal!

It was Cullen's *'Jansenism'* and *'Ultramontanism'* that spearheaded the *'Romanisation'* of the Catholic Church in Ireland and ushered in his own particular *'devotional revolution'* experienced in Ireland through the second half of the 19th century and much of the 20th century. All creating an exceptionally high, almost obsessive degree of religious observance and devotion, an equally exceptionally high, almost obsessive deference to priests and religious in general, an equally exceptionally high, almost obsessive adherence to Church rules, regulations and observances, and an equally high, almost obsessive culture of shame and guilt associated with the natural sexual act. Yes, a unique form of Catholicism, - Irish-style! Paul Cullen style!

Paul Cullen who made his entrance onto the Irish stage in 1849, after the Great Famine. Paul Cullen who believed that women's sexuality was an extreme threat, and therefore the *'virginity'* of Mary and Marian devotion were so central to his episcopate. Cullen who now established Irish Catholic Jansenism, which soon became so all-powerful.

And it was this insistence on abstaining from sex outside of marriage, instilled and infused into the Irish nation by Cullen, that brought about the *'Home Rule or Rome Rule'* crisis in 1890, over Charles Stewart Parnell, a protestant from Wicklow who was on the verge of achieving Home Rule for Ireland, but was *'scandalously'* involved with a married woman, Kitty O'Shea.

The Catholic Church came down heavily against Parnell. Archbishop after archbishop condemned him from the pulpit, calling for his resignation. And Parnell was taken down. The power of the Catholic Church to destroy a politician, who was not even a Catholic! The Catholic Church powerfully putting its own interests before the interests of the country! Had Home Rule come about with Parnell, the years of misery, pain and suffering inflicted on the Irish people in the 20th century would have been avoided! Our history would have been so different!

So it was not just the Catholic Church that Cullen controlled in Ireland! His frequent visits to the Viceregal Lodge were all made with the specific purpose of lobbying the Lord Lieutenant of Ireland and the government. The power of the Catholic Church extending into the political arena! Politics and religion continuing to be intertwined! Big time!

Cullen it was who moulded the Irish nation into a conservative, narrow-thinking, Victorian-minded people, obsessed with the *'evils'* of pre-marital sex, the desirability of chastity and purity outside of marriage, and hence early marriages and large families. Large families that only added to the impoverishment and economic depression!

Cullen it was who tore away the last lingering vestiges of the pagan beliefs, replacing their joyous celebrations and festivities, their free abandonment to the joys of the natural world and the natural uninhibited pleasures of the flesh with the imposition of rules, tensions and restraints. Hammering home that the old ways and festivities were now replaced by the new Christian ways: 1st February, St. Brigid's Day replacing Imbolc; 17th March, St Patrick's Day replacing Spring Equinox; 1st May, St Joseph's Day replacing Béaltine; 21st June, the feast of John the Baptist replacing Summer Solstice; 1st August, Loaf Mass (Lammas) replacing Lughnasadh; 29th September Michaelmas replacing Autumn Equinox; 1st November All Hallow's replacing Samhain and 25th December, Christmas Day, replacing Winter Solstice.

Cullen it was who changed the Irish Catholic Church with his set of Rome-inspired decrees in 1850 which directed it away from Celtic traditions and towards Victorian prudishness. Earning his brownie points for that elusive *'Red Hat'*!

And what was Cullen's legacy?

He is most notable today for being the first Irish cardinal. With his experience, connections and friendships in Rome he was able to influence the choice of appointments to episcopal sees in Australia, New Zealand, South Africa, and Canada. His relatives, friends, and students, referred to as *'Cullenites'*, exerted great influence overseas, with his nephew, Patrick Francis Moran, archbishop of Sydney, being a prime example. The term *'Cullenites'* is often also used when referring to a style of leadership resembling that of Cullen, characterised as *'authoritative'* and *'intransigent'*.

And one month after Cullen's death, on 27th November 1878, the occasion of his '*Month's Mind'*, Father Thomas N. Burke, O.P. in a sermon at a solemn Requiem Mass, eulogised him in no uncertain terms:

'The guiding spirit animating, encouraging and directing the wonderful work of the Irish Catholic Church for the last twenty eight years was Paul, Cardinal Cullen.'

Paul Cullen! On a mission to '*Romanise'* Ireland and bring all and sundry into line with the teachings, ethos and authority of Rome! Paul Cullen who established his own unique brand of Catholicism, - Irish-style! Based on Jansenism! And guess what? - He got his coveted '*red hat*'! Paul Cullen! - The first Irish Cardinal!

When Cullen died in 1879, after 29 years at the helm, Ireland was a backward, unprogressive country, economically depressed, a backwater, its people suffocated, infused and infested with narrow-minded religious observances.

Let us move forward into the 20th century now, to the other half of the '*Cullen/McQuaid*' duo! John Charles McQuaid, Archbishop of Dublin and Primate of all Ireland 1940-1972. John Charles McQuaid! - Archbishop of Dublin, the '*Catholic ruler of Ireland*' as his biographer John Cooney referred to him in the title of his book *'John Charles McQuaid - Ruler of Catholic Ireland*', and often referred to by historians as the '*biggest bogeyman in twentieth century Ireland*'. Sean O'Casey termed him '*the archdruid of Drumcondra'* as he sat there writing letters, - an acknowledgement of McQuaid's vast amount of correspondence, and how he was able to administer so much from that palace in Drumcondra, and not just in Church matters, but also in State affairs. Known in the Vatican under the code name '*Father X', and* referred to by Cardinal D'Alton at the centenary of Clonliffe College as '*the illustrious McQuaid*'.

John Charles McQuaid who continued the system established by Cullen in the previous century! The system that established and ensured the dominance of the Catholic Church in every aspect of life in Ireland! The system that was based on the ethos of this dominating and controlling Catholic Church, infused and imbued with Victorian prudishness, disgust of all matters pertaining to sexuality and instilling the belief that forgiveness and salvation could only be achieved through hard penance and physical suffering!

McQuaid, the control freak! McQuaid, with a finger in every pie! And McQuaid had very long fingers!

King Louis XIV of France was famous for his statement *L'Etat, c'est Moi!'* Meaning *'The State? - That's me! I am the State!'* Making very important decisions without consulting anyone else. The country under the control of a single individual and not the government of the people. So now too, in similar fashion, McQuaid claimed, *'Catholic Ireland? - That's me! I am Catholic Ireland!'*

McQuaid it was who dominated not just the Catholic Church in the 20th century, but the Irish State as well! Making Irish and Catholic synonymous! And as yet, still in his position as president of Blackrock College! Laying strong foundations for his future as the most powerful Catholic Church ruler! - *'I am Catholic Ireland!'*

McQuaid it was who, as president of Blackrock College and close to de Valera, became the chief architect and dictator of the new 1937 Irish Constitution! - McQuaid's crowning achievement! The Catholic Church recognised as having a special position in Catholic Ireland, although it stopped short of declaring Catholicism as the state religion. A Constitution that was described by many as more *'Catholic'* than *'Irish'*! The 1937 Constitution that placed a ban on abortion and divorce and would have included a ban on contraception if a law had not already been passed in 1935. The 1937 Constitution that delegated women's role to the home, McQuaid warning de Valera about *'Godless feminism'* and ordering women to leave all matters outside the home to their betters. The 1937 Constitution, with McQuaid's fingerprints all over it! The 1937 Constitution that made *'Irish'* and *'Catholic'* synonymous! Ireland now known world-wide as a wholly (holy!) Catholic country!

Under that 1937 Constitution, Church and State became one. A bonding of Church and State, for which McQuaid's episcopacy would become distinguished! No government measure able to be passed without the approval and input from McQuaid - *'I am Catholic Ireland!'*

McQuaid's belief and determination that the Church should be involved in politics, by Divine Right, to guide the faithful! His warning to the State about *'hands off'* as far as possible in private bodily matters, insisting it was not the State's place to be involved in people's personal lives. That was the Church's role, and he, McQuaid, therefore, as head of the Catholic Church in Ireland, controlled every aspect of daily life! - *'I am Catholic Ireland!'*

McQuaid put his stamp on absolutely everything! A control freak! And what was the **cause** of McQuaid being what he became? His biographer, John Cooney in his book *'John Charles McQuaid Ruler of Catholic Ireland'* published in 1999, explains:

'McQuaid's cold public image masked emotional scars from a tragic family background which were to shape his public life. These provide the framework for the relentless quest for respectability which was an integral part of McQuaid's adolescence and adult life, as well as contributing to his narrow devotionalism and excessive puritanism both as Dean of Studies and President of Blackrock College, and later as Archbishop of Dublin.' ('*John Charles McQuaid Ruler of Catholic Ireland*', John Cooney, page 14)

Cause and Effect! His tragic family background? - McQuaid's mother died just a week after he was born and his father married again a year later. McQuaid did not discover any of this until he was sixteen years old, and disclosed to him by a friend. And he was devastated! The woman he had always believed to be his mother now turned out to be his step-mother! An estrangement followed between McQuaid and his father and step-mother, which lasted for many years. And McQuaid's years spent at St. Patrick's

College Cavan were apparently far from happy, as he suffered serious ill health both physically and mentally, for whatever reason and for whatever he experienced while there. But after five years his father transferred him to Blackrock College and later to Clongowes Wood College. Later, the death of his half-brother Dean, to whom he had been close, killed in a Civil War ambush in County Mayo in February 1923, at the age of 26, was to be another devastating blow.

At nineteen years of age, he joined the religious order of the Holy Ghost Fathers, hoping to become a missionary in Africa. But priests in religious orders have a different kind of life, a different set of rules from diocesan priests. The superior of a religious order determines the rules, regulations and disciplines within his own monastery, each priest in his monastery bound by his oath of *'obedience'*, and wherever the superior decides to send him, that is where each priest will go, - just as each diocesan priest is directed to a certain parish by his bishop.

In joining the order of the Holy Ghost Fathers McQuaid was inducted into a life of hard penance, prayer, self-inflicted physical punishment, obligatory silence, and the orthodox belief that priests were a cut above ordinary mortals, and so were due a great deal of respect and a high degree of reverence. Taught that any sexual relationship outside of marriage was wrong and the most abhorrent of sins. Conditioned to accept, without questioning, that the Church was always right. In their male-only world, women represented a temptation and a threat to their all-important celibacy. Clerical students were expected to fall in line with Church teaching on sexuality, including its attitude towards unmarried mothers. And all of this McQuaid took with him into his role as the most powerful figure in the Catholic Church in Ireland. He was never sent to Africa! Those at the top of the Church pyramid, those in the upper echelons of the Vatican, the puppeteers who pulled all the strings, had him destined for Church greatness! But first he would serve as president in Blackrock College, run by the Holy Ghost Fathers.

Diarmaid Ferriter, lecturer in history in St. Patrick's College, Dublin City University, was born in Dublin in 1972. In his book *'The Transformation of Ireland 1900-2000'* published in 2004, Ferriter suggests that McQuaid's obsession with control was *'born of insecurity',* an insecurity revealed in his *'thorny relations'* with groups such as the Legion of Mary, founded by Frank Duff. Ferriter also refers to McQuaid as having an *'extraordinary arrogance',* and an ability to *'cause great irritation',* with his insecurity further revealed in his *'proud boasts'* that Ireland had more successfully than any other country *'resisted modern aberrations'.*

So again, the principle of **'cause and effect'**! It's always there! And in McQuaid's case? His desire for control coming from some form of insecurity reaching back into his childhood and his teenage years. And the effect of his austere training for the priesthood? - His belief that salvation could only come from repentance through physical punishment for sin. His relentless desire for control led him to interfere in, and stamp his authority on, every aspect of Irish life - *'I am Catholic Ireland'.* And his distrust of women? Coming from the revelation that the woman whom he believed to be his mother was in actual fact his step-mother! Betrayal! Betrayal by a woman! And all of this manifesting in the repressive and suppressive religious regime he imposed on Ireland during his reign.

McQuaid interfered in absolutely everything, including a lot which should have been none of his business! That's how he got so much power! He was involved in absolutely every aspect of life! But ironically it was this very interference which *'interfered'* in his achieving the coveted *'red hat'*, when the Vatican Minister to Ireland ensured McQuaid did not become a cardinal, by having a word in the pope's ear about just how arrogantly interfering McQuaid actually was.

And how exactly did McQuaid stamp his authority on all aspects of Irish life? To make *'Irish'* and *'Catholic'* synonymous? - By showing his hatred for all things non-Catholic, a hatred matched only by his hatred for unmarried mothers and their children! They were *'fallen women'* and their children the *'spawn of Satan', 'seed of the devil', 'bastards', 'illegitimate'*, and not fit to live in society.

- McQuaid sought to control all aspects of education, at all levels, including the various chairs of ethics, logic, education, sociology and psychology in University College Dublin and the appointment and dismissal of teachers in national and secondary schools. He insisted that every school in Ireland had religious instruction - based on his own Catechism, which became known as *'McQuaid's Catechism'* or *'McQuaid's green book'*. That's how powerful McQuaid was!

- In 1933, the Irish National Teachers' Organisation, INTO, put out a plan to establish an Educational Advisory Council which would give lay teachers a consultative role in school management and policy for the first time since the foundation of the Irish Free State in 1922. McQuaid was having none of it! Education was in safe Catholic Church hands, as he had set it up, with nuns, priests and religious orders, and that's how it would stay. That's how powerful McQuaid was!

- In 1934, McQuaid was scathing in his attack on women's athletics, declaring that women taking part in athletics with men, or even at the same venue as men, was gross, indecent, *'un-Catholic'* and *'un-Irish'*. Every Catholic college in Ireland sided with McQuaid in boycotting mixed athletics events. No surprise there! Think pyramid! Think control! Think fawning and bowing down to those at the top, to *'he who must be obeyed'*. That's how powerful McQuaid was!

- He proposed that the phrase *'for sale'* be removed from contraception pills. He wanted the Post Office to be able to open and search packages so that no contraceptions could be sent into Ireland for personal use from Britain or elsewhere.

- According to John Cooney, in his biography of McQuaid, *'John Charles*

McQuaid- Ruler of Catholic Ireland', McQuaid appeared at times to be acting '*more as a backbench Dail deputy',* for example, amongst others, intervening in the election of a home assistance officer in Clonmel, County Tipperary, the appointment of a doctor in Sixmilebridge County Clare, the possibility of securing a commercial contract for Roads and Roofs Ltd., and queries about the McHale Road housing scheme in Castlebar County Mayo. ('*John Charles McQuaid- Ruler of Catholic Ireland',* John Cooney, page 88) That's how powerful McQuaid was!

- He insisted that hospitals display the Crucifix in their wards, and promote all things Catholic to patients.

- He intervened in workers' strikes, which he described as '*the most potent form of social agitation'.*

- He spelt out the model of a traditional family as one based on a valid marriage, - a husband, a wife, with many children.

- He proposed that the state should encourage early marriages by providing tax allowances for children, promoting saving schemes and providing reasonably priced housing. Probably his most controversial input of all in the area of family was his establishing that the role of mothers was in the home.

- He made Blackrock College synonymous with national celebrations, such as the 1932 Eucharistic Congress which was held in Ireland.

- He asserted his authority, with a strict disciplinary code, over the priests and religious orders in his own diocese, forbidding them to buy cars, leave the diocese, renovate or expand their parochial houses, or publish articles in newspapers or periodicals without his personal approval.

- The distinguishing mark of a Catholic family was to be the nightly rosary.

- Girls were to be educated for their role of motherhood, - the divine vocation for most of them.

- Parents were to train their children in obedience, in preparation for them accepting obedience in all matters to the Catholic Church as they grew older. Parents were pivotal in the Catholic upbringing of their children, *'the instruction of their minds, the training of their wills to virtue, their bodily welfare, and their preparation of their life as a citizens. In the education of Catholics, every branch of human training was subject to the guidance of the Church, and those schools alone which the Church approved were capable of providing a fully Catholic education. Therefore, the Church forbade parents to send a child to any non-Catholic school whether primary or secondary, or continuation or university.'* And furthermore, the usual McQuaid threat, - *'Deliberately to disobey this law is a mortal sin, and they who persist in disobedience are unworthy to receive the Sacraments.'* (McQuaid's 1947 Easter Pastoral letter, as reported in the *Irish Times,* and quoted in *'A New Ireland',* Niall O'Dowd, page 143)

- He monitored closely the behaviour of university students, tightening the chaplaincy services at University College Dublin, insisting that students find suitable *'Catholic'* accommodation, and watching that they went to mass and on the annual pilgrimage to St. Patrick's Purgatory, Lough Derg in County Donegal. Salvation through penance and suffering and all that!

- He insisted that arranged soccer matches be called off on Good Friday to respect the sanctity of Holy Week.

- In January 1949, he expressed his displeasure that a Birmingham diocesan priest had been chosen to play for Ireland against France at

Lansdowne Road, which was in the Dublin diocese. He argued that priests who took part in public games in contravention of the Maynooth Statues were causing scandal.

- In 1955, he demanded that a soccer match between the Republic of Ireland and Yugoslavia be called off because his permission had not been sought, and also as a protest against the imprisonment of Cardinal Aloys Stepinac by Marshall Tito's Communist regime. The No. 1 army band cancelled its appointment to play at the match and RTE refused to broadcast. Those who did attend the match had to pass a picket of Legion of Mary members carrying anti-Communist placards. All in obedience to McQuaid! That's how powerful he was! But! This incident showed that he did not always get his own way! Because despite all his efforts, over 21,000 people defied him and turned up for the game, which went ahead.

- He insisted that the Angelus bell be broadcast twice daily on the national RTE as an observance of Catholic devotion.

- He meddled in the internal affairs of religious orders, as for example in his dealings with the Redemptorists, when they wanted to open a retreat house in the Dublin diocese.

- He interfered in the opening hours of pubs and insisted on Sunday closing, warning publicans who continued to sell alcohol on Sundays that they would be committing a mortal sin.

- He insisted that greyhound racing be stopped on Sundays. Also a mortal sin for those who indulged in it!

- He forbade burials of non-Catholics in those parts of cemeteries reserved for Catholics.

- He heavily influenced the Censorship Board, determining which newspapers, television programmes and literature to which people should have access. Very often he even objected to a particular music request that was played live over the radio on *'Hospitals' Requests'*, where relatives of those in hospital could phone in on the live programme and request a particular song to be played. John Cooney in his biography of McQuaid, relates how on one occasion, a Cole Porter number *'Always True to You'* was played. McQuaid objected to the words *'But I'm always true to you / Darling in my fashion. / I'm always true to you in my way.'* Harmless words indeed, one would think! But not McQuaid! After the programme was over, the presenter, Tom Cox, was called into the director general's office and told how His Grace was very concerned at the morality of the song. And why? Because, according to McQuaid, it sent out the message that a limited form of fidelity was somehow acceptable!

- McQuaid's interference and control in censorship resulted in many Irish writers being censored, and having to leave the country. John McGahon was just one example. He lost his job as a primary school teacher in Clontarf after the banning of his second novel *'The Dark'*, as a result of McQuaid using his influence with the INTO to ensure that McGahon be removed from his position.

- McQuaid strongly objected to what was called *'pulp fiction'* at the time, disgusted and dismayed that it was rotting the nation's soul, with glossy sexually suggestive covers, sold at all airports, bus and train stations and street newspaper stalls.

- He insisted on having a say in the type of habit worn by nuns, and where they went on holidays.

- On an Aer Lingus flight to Lourdes, he noticed that on the back of the menu, there was a map of Dublin, sponsored by Guinness's brewery, showing places of interest such as Christ Church Cathedral, Trinity College, - all Protestant landmarks, no Catholic ones. The Aer Lingus sales manager was promptly informed of McQuaid's displeasure.

- No Catholics were allowed, by Catholic Church orders, to attend the Protestant Trinity College, under threat of excommunication.

- His vast network of spies kept him informed of all that was happening both in society and inside all government departments. He knew everything that was going on! That's how he got so much control! Don't forget! - Knowledge is power! And the Catholic Church gained knowledge through the confessional box and through the visits of the priest to the home! All private, personal and family matters disclosed to the priest!

- He interfered in the adoption process of young babies to America, which began around 1947. These babies were the babies of unmarried mothers, *'fallen women'* as the Church called them, babies mostly born in the Magdalene Homes and taken from their mothers at birth or very soon afterwards. It was McQuaid who insisted that prospective adoptive American parents sign an affidavit, pledging to raise the child as a Catholic. He allowed the trafficking to America to continue, demanding that the State have no say in what he claimed was the Church's business. Children taken from their mothers and sold to the highest bidder! How much lower could it possibly get?

- McQuaid's hatred for unmarried mothers saw them condemned to incarceration within Magdalene institutions. Many of them the victims of rape, incest and sexual abuse and rape by priests and bishops. Many of them who, when they reported the abuse inflicted upon them, were themselves taken away to face punishment, while the perpetrators of the abuse were left to continue their life unscathed.

McQuaid! - Self-designated judge, jury and executioner all in one! McQuaid! Anti-everything that was not under the control of the Catholic Church! A Catholic Church in turn that was totally under **his** control! - *'I am Catholic Ireland*'!

But! Despite all his endeavours, there was no evidence of a decline in alcohol consumption or a rise in higher moral standards!

McQuaid loved the ceremonial aspect of his Catholic Church episcopacy, the '*gear*' as he called all the different dressage, ceremonial attire and paraphernalia. Arrogant in his estimation of his own importance, he is reported to have instructed his chauffeur to drive round and round again until all other dignitaries had arrived at the venue, and then he would enter the last of all. He insisted on being the first person to greet President JFK on the tarmac at Dublin airport, arguing that the airport was in the Dublin Diocese and therefore his territory. And he is reported as arriving at the theatre at very opportune moments, such as when he arrived at a performance of Handel's '*Messiah*'. The lights were already dimmed, and then McQuaid entered in his splendid red robes to take his place in the distinguished visitors' box to the chant in Latin of '*Ecce Homo*' - Here comes the man. - An opportune moment or what! He insisted on the kissing of his Borgia ring and the bowing of the knee to him on all public occasions, as well as congregations and assembled audiences rising to their feet when he entered, and on the wearing of formal dress by staff when he visited hospitals and other public establishments. - '*I am Catholic Ireland*'!

Without any pastoral experience, McQuaid's managerial style was that of a headmaster, learned in his years spent in that role in Blackrock College, with those who pleased him and deferred to him receiving rewards, those who disobeyed or opposed him being punished or dismissed to the sidelines. Strongly imbued with a sense of the extreme importance and dignity of his office, he expected and demanded total deference and obedience.

And on top of all this dominant and unquestionable control over people's lives, McQuaid waged a further campaign against any and every undenominational or community-led service, getting them closed down through insisting on withdrawal of council or other sources of funding, unless they agreed to come under his own personal jurisdiction and supervision. Such an example was the

St. John Ambulance Brigade, a non-denominational organisation, in their scheme to promote women's health, which McQuaid succeeded in getting cancelled, forcing Dublin Corporation to cut its annual funding to the organisation.

And the grounds on which Dublin Corporation explained their actions? It would not be pleasing or acceptable to the ecclesiastical authorities! In other words, McQuaid would not be pleased! It obviously did not matter to McQuaid or concern him in the least the good work such organisations were doing, - all that mattered to him was having power and control over them!

And an internal 1950 memo of the Department of External Affairs, quoted on page 18 in Mike Milotte's book *'Banished Babies'*, reads:

'We shall have to be careful not to do anything which would embarrass the Archbishop'.

And the title *'His Grace Is Displeased'* is indeed a suitable one for the book, edited by Clara Cullen and Margaret Ó hÓgartaigh, containing selected correspondence of John Charles McQuaid, from his own archives.

A subservient government! Subservient to the Catholic Church under McQuaid! And how did that happen? How did the situation develop, where the Irish State bowed down to the demands of the Catholic Church?

Simply because, as already explained in this chapter, the Catholic Church, first under Paul Cullen and then under John Charles McQuaid, had so much control over the everyday lives of the Irish nation, a control established through instilling fear and guilt, a control established through dictating what was acceptable moral behaviour, a control established through instilling into the Irish psyche a totally thwarted attitude toward the sexual act and a disgust towards and a rejection of those women who infringed against the moral, sexual codes laid down by the Catholic Church, and fear of the societal shame and guilt that inevitably accompanied such an infringement. Catholicism Irish-style! Based on Jansenism!

But the question that needs to be answered is, - how exactly were they able to do this? How was this made possible? How did they ever get away with it all?

This was all possible because the Catholic Church under McQuaid controlled all aspects of education, health and social services! Every aspect of daily life! Education in particular!

Education! Education! Education! The chief propaganda mechanism of the Catholic Church in Ireland! The Catholic Church was educating a new generation of politicians and administrators – all in its own model, - often through such as the Christian Brothers, moulding the youth of Ireland in the Catholic Church fashion, into a particular brand. And these in turn all owed allegiance and loyalty to those who created them! To those who helped them up the pyramid!

And how exactly did that come about? How did the Catholic Church get total control of education?

Simply because there was another person in this equation! - Eamon de Valera! A devout Catholic!

The same Eamon de Valera, whom Tim Pat Coogan in his biography of de Valera in 1993, *'De Valera, long fellow, long shadow',* explains how historians were later apt to depict him as a *'sort of lay cardinal, at one level expressing and symbolizing Ireland's interface between church and state .....a Church whose rule as a layman he dutifully followed in most aspects of his waking life'* and who also, according to Coogan, helped to create a *'political church-state monolith'* and was *'primarily a Catholic head of government'*. (Diarmaid Ferriter, *'Judging Dev'* page 218)

Paul Cullen - John Charles McQuaid - Eamon de Valera!

Cullen dead but not quite gone! Now living on in the *'holy alliance'* formed between McQuaid and Eamon de Valera, between Church and State, that raised the question as to who exactly was running the country! Church or State? From Dail Eireann, with its elected representatives of the Irish people, or from the Archbishop's palace in Drumcondra in north Dublin and his secluded mansion in Killiney, with its spectacular and uninterrupted views over Dublin Bay?

Eamon De Valera! The other half of this *'holy'* or *'unholy'* alliance, - whichever you prefer to call it, - between Church and State!

The same Eamon de Valera whose political career spanned and dominated the dramatic period of Ireland's modern cultural and national revolution in the half century following the country's newly established independence.

The same Eamon de Valera, self-styled and self-proclaimed father figure of the Irish nation.

The same Eamon De Valera, credited by many with the vision of Ireland as *'comely maidens dancing at the cross roads',* and a society founded on the family unit, where women were wives and mothers, fulfilling their domestic role. A society where pregnancy and giving birth outside of marriage was repugnant and shameful, a society where any form of contraception was forbidden, and a society where divorce was totally prohibited.

McQuaid and de Valera were indeed well matched!

And indeed it was not just de Valera who bowed down to McQuaid! So too did John Costello, the Fine Gael lawyer who headed two Inter-Party Governments. Costello, who supported McQuaid in opposing the Dr. Noel Browne when Browne, as Minister of Health, tried to introduce a non-means tested scheme for mother and baby welfare. Costello had kept McQuaid informed about all the relevant cabinet discussions, McQuaid condemning Browne's attempt as *'socialised medicine'*. Costello supplied each member of the cabinet with a copy of McQuaid's statement, signed by all the Irish bishops, but clearly all McQuaid's work. In the face of combined Church opposition, and government deference to McQuaid, Browne had no cabinet support and was forced to resign. All reminiscent of the previous taking down of Parnell by Cullen in 1890. Browne himself commented:

'My most powerful and uncompromising opponent was Dr John Charles McQuaid'.

McQuaid had actually previously *'summoned'* Browne to his palace, in July 1950, - the very act of *'summoning'* a government minister indicative of McQuaid's power and self-designated authority. And within his own palace walls, on his own home territory, McQuaid admonished Browne, in no uncertain terms. He objected especially to the fact that doctors trained in non-Catholic hospitals would be treating Catholic patients. And worst of all, gynaecologists not trained in Catholic hospitals examining women's breasts and vaginas! Intolerable! Totally unacceptable! Unthinkable! Not going to happen! Such medical officers did not, and could not understand Catholic principles! And giving advice to women and young girls on sexual relations, marriage, maybe even advising them on abortion and contraception! Non-Catholic doctors should never be allowed to be in that position!

McQuaid certainly held a *'moral monopoly'.* A moral monopoly that later Taoiseachs were unwilling to challenge! Sean Lemass, in the 1960s, and his successor, Jack Lynch, were both hesitant about going against McQuaid. Lynch gave into McQuaid when McQuaid urged him not to give into removing the ban on contraception.

John Charles McQuaid! He who served not just as an archbishop with total power and control over Church matters in the lives of the Irish Catholic nation, but also as de Valera's right hand man, with almost total control over State matters as well. Believing that the Church and not the State, had the Divine Right to be involved in people's personal and private bodily matters.

John Charles McQuaid who loomed large over all and every aspect of Irish life, as Archbishop of Dublin from 1940 to 1972, - *'I am Catholic Ireland!'*

McQuaid's forced resignation in December 1971 has been described as a watershed, not only in the life of the Catholic Church in Ireland, but also in Irish politics and society. He had his supporters and his opponents. Praised on the one hand for his *'outstanding service to the Church'*, for his *'personal kindness'* and all his good works helping society, for being a *'distinguished scholar'*, an *'educationalist', and* for his genuine desire to protect his flock from contaminating outside influences. On the other hand, criticised for his interference, his desire for control in all matters, his unrelenting opposition to all things non-Catholic, his strict adherence to Church policies, his Victorian prudishness, and his intolerance of unmarried women.

However, underneath all this veneer of Victorian prudishness, *'decency'*, *'respectability'* and *'holiness'* there lurked dark and sinister secrets!

It was John Charles McQuaid who handled the first ever allegations of child abuse against a priest, named as Father Edmondus. And his particular irresponsible handling of that case dictated how future such cases would be dealt with by the Catholic Church hierarchy! It was McQuaid who established the pattern, set the precedent, adhered to even to this present day, of not holding to account those priests or bishops guilty of child sex abuse or rape. When he made the decision to sweep the Edmondus allegations under the carpet both the State and clergy followed his lead. That's how powerful he was!

Powerful enough indeed for the Gardai to be intimidated by him, handing over reports about Edmondus to him without even investigating them for themselves. The Gardai clearly regarded priests as being outside of their remit!

Edmondus had been sexually abusing young children between the ages of eight and eleven in Our Lady's Hospital for Sick Children in Crumlin in the late 1950s and early 1960s. One of the young girls whom Edmondus had raped was

And the Walls Came Tumbling Down!

Marie Collins, who later became a powerful advocate for victims of sexual abuse. She was chosen to meet Pope Frances to explain the Irish clerical abuse situation to him. It took 36 years before Edmondus faced justice, sentenced to just 18 months in prison and released in May 1998.

Edmondus! - Jimmy Saville and Rolf Harris, - Irish-style! And just as their multiple crimes against young children were swept under the carpet, so too, McQuaid turned a blind eye to the horrendous crimes of Edmondus. Even though he was informed by the Gardai that Edmondus had taken sexually explicit photographs of two girls at the hospital, he handed the case over to his auxiliary bishop, Bishop Dunne, who found that a crime had indeed been committed under canon law. But McQuaid reversed the decision, and in one of his interminable written notes, explained how he felt that Edmondus '*clearly understood the nature of the sinful act involved and to send him on retreat would defame him*'.

And unbelievable as it is, he accepted the false, fabricated explanation put forward by Edmondus that coming from a family of only brothers and no sisters, he was just curious about female genitalia!

And why did McQuaid choose to accept this explanation? Could it be because he himself was obsessed with female genitalia? Clearly indicated by his demanding that tampons should be banned, because, he claimed, by inserting them, women were being artificially sexually stimulated! And how, one must ask, could McQuaid possibly have known about anything to do with tampons? And when it was reported that he used a magnifying glass to show the proprietor of the Irish Press newspaper that in one of his advertisements for ladies' underwear, a woman's '*mons veneris*' was visible! And when he was being driven past Cleary's department store in O'Connell Street in Dublin, he objected to the nude models in the window being visible while their dressage was being changed. Certainly McQuaid had an unnatural and unhealthy preoccupation with the '*evils*' of sex, again suggesting his discomfort around women and in many ways his own personal repression, indeed being described by many as *'enormously repressed sexually'*. He is reported as seeking out *'dirty books'*, or *'foul books'* for himself to read. And his excuse? - in order to judge them to see if they needed to be banned! His biographer, John Cooney in his book *'John Charles McQuaid - Ruler of Catholic Ireland'* tells how Mrs. Mercy Simms, wife of the Protestant Archbishop George Simms, who worked with McQuaid on opening a school for travellers' children, spoke out about how McQuaid had what seemed to be an unhealthy attraction towards boys and very frequently sought to have them around him. Cooney further relates how McQuaid lectured to boys all the time about masturbation:

'According to the teachings of the Church, not only was masturbation deemed to be a sin; it also caused blindness. McQuaid was convinced that the Catholic Church had a duty to supply instruction in chastity that was accurate, clear, adequate and supernatural. 'It can be done without hurt to sensitivity and without physical details', he told a mental health conference at the St. John of God hospital in Stillorgan. 'I am equally convinced that very many neuroses have their origin in the defective training in chastity.' (*'John Charles McQuaid Ruler of Catholic Ireland'*, John Cooney page 284)

McQuaid's handling of the Edmondus case showed clearly that his main priorities were avoidance of scandal, protecting the reputation of the Catholic Church, and preserving the secrecy surrounding such matters. All other considerations, such as justice for the victims or the welfare of children were subordinate to these priorities. He even went against the Catholic Church's own canon law and did his best to avoid any application of State law. And that was the precedent he established! A precedent still being followed! As we all know!

And why did McQuaid act in such a way, covering up clerical child abuse? Could it be because he himself was sexually abusing and raping young boys? Could that be the reason? - Just asking!

Certainly, after his death in 1973, he was named in the Murphy Commission as having raped and sexually abused young boys over a number of years. Reports also circulated about the scale of rape and sexual abuse that went on at his Boys Club in Eccles Street in Dublin, known later as Our Lady's Hostel, in the 1960s and 1970s, a hostel for boys, opened in the early 1960s and run by nuns on behalf of the Archdiocese, which was reputed to have been visited by *'hundreds'* of men of the holy cloth! It typically housed up to 30 teenage boys, aged 15 to 18, in dormitories.

The Irish Sunday Mirror, 7th July 2019, published an article by Sylvia Pownall, Editor, on the Gardai probe which uncovered evidence of a paedophile ring run by clerics. Claims of clerical sex abuse at this same Dublin *'hostel of horrors'*, where victims claimed priests passed them around *'like pieces of meat'*, were investigated by officers attached to the Sexual Crime Management Unit. The perpetrators included the evil predator Brendan Smyth, suspected of abusing more than 140 children over a 40-year period.

The report cited evidence from various victims of sex abuse and rape by priests, including senior clergy. The boys were bribed with cigarettes and money to keep quiet, one man claiming he was also warned on several occasions to *'keep his mouth shut'* or he would *'end up in the lunatic asylum in Dundrum'*. According to the report, a typical ploy used by senior clerics was to send their car and chauffeur to the hostel to collect a particular boy who would then be driven to a nearby location and abused.

The same report confirmed that more than 700 vulnerable teenage boys passed through the hostel over the space of a decade and it was feared most were preyed on by clerics. Abusers included seminarians and their foreign visitors from Clonliffe, All Hallows and Maynooth as well as visiting priests and their *'guests'*.

'They all wanted to be our friends, to buy us stuff like ciggies, drink, food, movies or take us out on drives in the country for sex in their cars'.

The New York Times, on December 8th, 2011 reported:

'The main body of the Murphy report was highly critical of Archbishop McQuaid's attitude toward abuse, accusing him of showing 'no concern for the welfare of children'. However, this is the first suggestion that the official body had received specific complaints against Archbishop McQuaid, who was at the very apex of the Roman Catholic Church in Ireland for three decades.

In a statement, a victims' group, One in Four, called for a statutory inquiry into the accusations, saying that 'if Archbishop McQuaid was, as is alleged, a sex offender himself, then it is no wonder that the secrecy and cover-ups which have characterized the church's handling of sexual abuse was so entrenched'.

And it was during McQuaid's watch that the notorious Magdalene Institutions flourished in Ireland. The Magdalene Institutions! Mother-and-Baby homes, laundries and asylums! A deliberate campaign of venom and viciousness waged against any and every female in society who was deemed undesirable by the misogynistic standards of the Catholic Church! McQuaid's hatred of women, in particular unmarried mothers, playing out in full force! True, - McQuaid did not establish the Magdalene Institutions. They were already in operation before he was even ordained to the priesthood. So he cannot be blamed for that! But it was during his watch, in the 1940s, 50s and 60s that they flourished and prospered, and he did nothing to stop it! And the Industrial Schools!

So, to recap! All the dominance and control, first by Cullen in the 19th century, and then carried on by McQuaid in the 20th century, in every aspect of Irish life, and especially through their monopoly on education, explains how the Catholic Church in Ireland achieved such a dominant position in the every-day lives of the Irish nation. The Catholic Church under McQuaid controlled education, health and social services through a nation-wide network of Catholic-run hospitals and schools. And in the new Irish Free State, in the *'holy alliance'* between Church and State, between Eamon de Valera, a devout Catholic, and McQuaid, in the running of those schools and hospitals, the Catholic Church demanded that the State supplied the necessary financial funding, but at the same time, the Catholic Church, in the person of McQuaid, further demanded that the State had no control or no input into any of these institutions, - all that was to be the sole preserve of the Catholic Church! All under McQuaid!

The collusion between Church and State! The State's public purse funded education, healthcare and social welfare services. And the Catholic Church, under McQuaid, held all control and power within those various establishments. McQuaid was on a winner!

The Church used the State, and the State used the Church! In a mutually benefitting *'Holy alliance'*!

And what did the Irish State gain from this *'holy alliance'*? - Stability and continuity, amid all the uncertainties of the 1920s and 1930s, when the new State was struggling to establish new institutions of education, health and social welfare, never having had such experience before. And right there was McQuaid! The man of the moment! The educationalist, president of the prestigious Blackrock College! President of the Catholic Association of Headmasters! McQuaid who had established himself as a great organiser, as in his organisation of the 1932 International Eucharistic Congress, held in Ireland, with Blackrock College in the limelight! McQuaid, the Church administrator! McQuaid, the reformer! McQuaid the theologian! McQuaid, the pioneer of social services! McQuaid, the builder of schools and hospitals! And this very same McQuaid right there now on the spot! No better man for the task of organising the education system of this new nation! Stability and continuity by handing over to the Catholic Church responsibility for the nation's moral fibre, by enshrining significant elements of the Catholic moral code in law, particularly in the areas of sexual morality and family relations.

And what did the Catholic Church gain? - Control! In all areas of life!

The result of this *'holy'* alliance was that most of one's day was spent under either the direct or the indirect supervision of the Catholic clergy, between school, hospital, social services, and the various on-going religious observances and rituals, - Sunday and daily mass, weekly confessional, devotions, nightly rosary, benediction, days of fast and abstinence, Lenten services, observance of the sacraments, Confirmation, Baptism, etc. etc. etc.

And of course, the knowledge the priests had of people's everyday lives! Through visits to the homes and through the confession box! They knew everything about everybody! And all fed back to McQuaid! Through his network of spies, his *'eyes',* his *'ears'* everywhere, watching, listening!

And a Catholic Church that was able to exert so much control over people's everyday lives, - that same Catholic Church held the power of the ballot box, the power of the public vote in its hands. And every government is totally dependent on the public vote! In just the same way as every American president is determined to find Irish roots, - in order to win the vote of the Irish-American Catholics! And without that, no president can win the White House!

Testimony to McQuaid's success in all his *'Romanising'* endeavours was evident when, after the 1963 visit to Ireland of the Catholic President Kennedy, almost every house, cottage, and bed and breakfast establishment in Ireland exhibited a framed picture of the Sacred Heart, complete with a constantly lit lamp, and a picture of both the pope and Kennedy alongside it. And often a rosary beads strung over all.

And so, yes indeed, *'Irish'* and *'Catholic'* had become synonymous. But the *'Catholicism'* was a uniquely *'Irish-style'* brand! Loyalty and adherence to the Catholic Church was based on entrapment. And fear coming from that entrapment!

Fear! - That most lethal of weapons in any arsenal! And no institution was able to use it better than the Catholic Church did in Ireland!

Church monopoly! Nobody able or willing to stand up against the power and authority of the Catholic Church! Fear of a resounding hit with that bishop's mitre! That bishop's mitre that loomed threateningly over everyone!

Yes, Irish people saw themselves as Catholic in the 20th century. Catholicism, Irish-style certainly played a central role in Irish identity. It was not something that they **did,** nor was it something that they **had,** - it was simply what they **were**! It was a **way of life**! It was in their **thinking**! They **lived and breathed** it! From the high-and-mighty in society right down to the not-so-high-and-mighty! De Valera himself a devout Catholic; Taoiseach John Costello with a private chapel in his Dublin home; the entire Dáil attending Mass at 6am on September 1939, having spent the night debating, and voting on Irish neutrality; the priest called to the bedside of every dying person; the priest involved in all aspects of life, from the cradle to the grave and everything in between; the blessing of a new car, a new house, the Aer Lingus fleet, the fishing fleet, etc.; pilgrimages to holy sites, novenas, etc; the holy water font inside the door of every home; the sprinkling of holy water as everyone left the house; the constant signing of the cross; the constant supplications *'Please God', 'God bless';* the wearing of miraculous medals, etc; the carrying of the rosary beads - as Constance Markievicz lay dying in 1927, she had the rosary beads entwined in her hands. - All testimony to how central Catholicism was to people's lives!

And a long line of political figures, from Michael Collins to Jack Lynch and Charlie Haughey, all boastful of having a brother a priest, or a sister a nun. The wow factor for any family! And President Mary Robinson, - openly talking about how she was inspired in her public service role by her two aunts who were missionary nuns.

That was then, this is now! And now, today? McQuaid's dominance and control over matters both spiritual and political, mean very little indeed to the younger generation of Irish people who have grown up dancing to a different tune, and for whom Irish and Catholic are no longer synonymous. A younger generation who follow their own likes in music, literature, art, theatre, television programmes, drama, irrespective of Church dogma or teachings. A younger generation who would never tolerate the Church interfering in their personal and private lives! A younger generation who would never seek or adhere to advice from the priest telling them what to do! Those days are long gone!

And to finish this chapter! Hitler made Germany synonymous with Nazism. Nazism that controlled every aspect of people's lives in Germany, through bullying, intimidation and instilling fear. And McQuaid? McQuaid made Ireland synonymous with Catholicism in exactly the same way, by controlling every aspect of people's lives through bullying, intimidation and instilling fear.

See the similarity?

And the Jews! We know how Hitler felt about the Jews. And McQuaid? How did he feel?

Strongly and vehemently anti-Semitic, McQuaid believed that Jews, along with Communists, Freemasons and Protestants were responsible for the world-wide struggle going on between Satan and the good angels. The good angels being the Catholic Church leaders, and the Jews at the front of the attacks against the Church. Modern movies such as *'King of Kings', 'Ben Hur',* and *'The Ten Commandments'* were criticised by McQuaid as showing Jesus only as a man, not as the divine being the Catholic Church believed him to be. And depicting him as a member of the Jewish race! Abhorrent to McQuaid! He was outspoken and clear in his attacks:

'From the first persecutions till the present moment, you will find Jews engaged in practically every movement against Our Divine Lord and his Church..........A Jew as a Jew is utterly opposed to Jesus Christ and all the Church means. But further, Satan has other allies; all those who by deliberate revolt against God and his Church set themselves under the government and direction of the Evil One. I want you to remember the truth very clearly: by Satan we mean not only Lucifer and the fallen Angels, but also those men, Jews or others, who by

deliberate revolt against Our Divine Lord have chosen Satan for their head.'
(McQuaid's words in 1932, before he became archbishop of Dublin in 1940)

Ring any bells?

Chapter 3:

Society in 20th-century Ireland -

The image and the reality

First of all, the image. The image portrayed by the Irish Tourist Association, from 1925, in promoting Ireland as a tourist destination. This newly independent Irish nation was open for business! Open for tourists! A promotional image that gathered momentum right up to the 1980s. Contrary to the common perception that Irish tourism began in the 1960s, the advertising and promotion of Ireland as a tourist destination actually dates back to the late 19th century.

The Emerald Isle! A glittering jewel set in clear, sparkling waters, - the Irish Sea on one side, the wild Atlantic Ocean on the other! The green fields of Erin! A magical, mythical land! A land of legends, imagination and mystery! The land of one hundred thousand welcomes! A magic land where time stood still! The unspoilt scenic attractions, the rugged coastlines, the unsullied beaches, the picturesque thatched cottages, the legendary and mysterious Giant's Causeway, the Glens of Antrim, the world-renowned Lakes of Killarney with those unique jaunting cars, the spectacular Cliffs of Moher, the captivating Glens of Wicklow, the natural wonder of the Burren in County Clare, the peace and quiet of Connemara, the awe-inspiring Rock of Cashel, little enchanting villages dotted here and there, monastic sites, castles and round towers holding secrets of an ancient past......and so it went on! All bolstered up with such iconic films as *'Ryan's Daughter'* and *'The Quiet Man'*. And of course, shamrocks, leprechauns and that inevitable pint of Guinness!

An idyllic spot on the western seaboard of Europe, untouched by the modern advancements and commercialisation that had gripped the rest of the world!

And the Walls Came Tumbling Down!

A charming atmosphere of timelessness, peace and tranquillity, where the traveller could replenish the soul, recharge the spiritual batteries, renew his zest for life, and throw all cares and caution to the wind!

A happy-go-lucky, friendly people, with that charming Irish smile! The captivating beat of Irish music, the intoxicating twirl of Irish dancing feet! The lure of the welcoming local pub with its drowning of sorrows and that get-away-from-it-all promise! Sure who would not want to come to Ireland?

We all know that every society, every generation, every political party, every world leader, - they all use and abuse history for their own ends, to match their own particular agenda. It's all part of the game! Part of the game being played out on this low third dimension energy-level playing field we call Earth. And we all know it is the winners who write the history books! And so it is with the jewel in Ireland's crown! - St. Patrick!

St. Patrick, - he who got a vision of the Irish people calling to him from across the water! St. Patrick, - he whom most people in Ireland believe was Catholic! St. Patrick - whose main claim to fame in most people's minds is getting rid of all those non-existent snakes!

St. Patrick's Day! That one day in the year when the whole world wants to be Irish! That day that generates millions of pounds, euros and dollars into the Irish economy!

The Ireland so poignantly projected by Eamon de Valera in his 1943 St. Patrick's Day speech *'On Language and the Irish Nation'*, delivered to the Irish people over the radio, when he spoke of the *'ideal Ireland that we would have, the Ireland that we dreamed of'*.

And who is the *'we'* referred to here by de Valera? De Valera who was not even Irish, but American!

And what sort of Ireland was de Valera portraying? ? In his own words:

'............the home of a people who valued material wealth only as a basis for right living, of a people who, satisfied with frugal comfort, devoted their leisure to the things of the spirit – a land whose countryside would be bright with cosy homesteads, whose fields and villages would be joyous with the sounds of industry, with the romping of sturdy children, the contest of athletic youths and the laughter of happy maidens, whose firesides would be forums for the wisdom of serene old age. The home, in short, of a people living the life that God desires that men should live. With the tidings that make such an Ireland possible, St. Patrick came to our ancestors fifteen hundred years ago promising happiness here no less than happiness hereafter. It was the pursuit of such an Ireland that later made our country worthy to be called the island of saints and scholars. It was the idea of such an Ireland – happy, vigorous, spiritual – that fired the imagination of our poets..........'

Holy Catholic Ireland! The isle of saints and scholars! The Ireland of one hundred thousand welcomes! And of course, that so often misquoted line in de Valera's speech *'Comely maidens dancing at the crossroads'*! The projected image of a devout Catholic nation!

But! Reality check!

That was the surface, the veneer! The image presented! In reality? - An Ireland that never existed! An Ireland of de Valera's unattainable vision!

In the stark light of reality, mid-20th century Ireland was not a place of magic, care-free days, contentment and peace of mind. Far from it! With John Charles McQuaid and Eamon de Valera at the helm, in their *'holy alliance'* between Church and State, they created a politically isolated Ireland, closed off from other countries. Strict censorship in all literature, in all areas of the media, - television, radio, films, documentaries, - to keep Ireland socially and culturally pure and free from all contaminating outside influences, in particular those influences emanating from Ireland's nearest neighbours on boths sides, capitalist America on the one side and Protestant Britain on the other, - resulting only in a stifling, suffocating, repressed nation, obsessed with sexual prudishness, Catholic Church morality and imposed codes of conduct. Guilt-ridden and fearful! Fearful of the threats of hell and eternal damnation! Fearful of what the Church could do to you! All part of the propaganda machine of the Catholic Church! Propaganda easily imposed on an uneducated people! Easily imposed on a people cut off from all external influences!

A small, isolated, closed, backward agrarian country with a mostly rural population, a depressed economy with no prospect of jobs, with large families as a result of early marriages due to the Catholic Church prohibition on contraception and their teaching on sex outside of marriage being filthy, a sin, an abhorrent crime! Shameful and disgusting! The only way to circumnavigate all of this was emigration. And the boats were full!

As Enda Kenny said in his speech, in the apology he issued as Taoiseach, in the Dail on Tuesday 19th February 2013, to all those who had suffered at the hands of religious orders in the Magdalene and State institutions:

'As I read this report and as I listened to these women, it struck me that for generations Ireland had created a particular portrait of itself as a good-living, God-fearing nation. Through this and other reports we know this flattering self-portrait to be fictitious.

Yes, by any standards it was a cruel, pitiless Ireland, distinctly lacking in a quality of mercy. That much is clear, both from the ages of the report, and from the stories of the women I met.

As I sat with these women, as they told their stories, it was clear that while every woman's story was different, each of them shared a particular experience of a particular Ireland - judgemental, intolerant, petty and grim.

We lived with the damaging idea that what was desirable and acceptable in the eyes of the Church and the State was the same and interchangeable........'

What a marked contrast! What a marked contrast between the earlier idyllic image put out by the Irish Tourist Board and Eamon de Valera, and the real image as explained by Enda Kenny in his role as Taoiseach many decades later! And the harshness of that reality!

What a marked contrast between the idyllic image put out by the the Irish Tourist Board and Eamon de Valera, and what our own social commentators were telling us! Our own writers, dramatists and poets! And again, the harshness of that reality!

So whom do we trust? The Tourist Board promotional literature? De Valera's romantic but unattainable image? Or our own writers, dramatists and poets?

As early as the mid 18th century, travellers from other countries had been attracted to Ireland, providing an insight into Irish society and culture, and people '*drinking whiskey, porter and punch*'. Travellers and writers such as Maria Wakefield, Mr. and Mrs. Hall, Thomas Reid, John Barrow, to mention just a few. All describing a peasant class steeped in poverty, sloth, misery, ignorance, and with a fighting nature!

Let us fast forward now to the 19th and 20th centuries!

19th Century Ireland! A '*Romanised*' Ireland! An Ireland brought into line with Rome by Cardinal Paul Cullen, and his '*devotional revolution'* imposed on the Irish people! A Paul Cullen whose beliefs were based on Jansenism and Ultramontanism, all explained in the previous chapter.

And now 20th century Ireland! An Ireland where Cullen's work was carried on, cemented and rubber-stamped by John Charles McQuaid! An Ireland where Church and State worked together in the '*holy alliance*' between McQuaid and De Valera! And again, all explained in the previous chapter. In mid-20th century, Ireland was a solidly Catholic country and the Church's authority was unquestioned, at least in public. It was still a predominantly rural society as well. Church and State were as one in their determination to enforce a deeply traditional moral code, and in the process, they displayed what many would see today as an unhealthy obsession with sexual matters, seeking to extend their authority into the bedrooms of the nation. Artificial birth control was outlawed and chastity was demanded of everyone who wasn't married.

This was the Ireland of James Joyce's *'The Dubliners'*, the Ireland of Patrick Kavanagh's novel *'Tarry Flynn'* and his poem *'The Great Hunger'*, the Ireland of Brian Friel's drama *'Philadelphia, Here I Come!'*, the Ireland of Edna O'Brien and Bryan MacMahon.

It is through literature, and not our history books, that we get the clearest view and understanding of society down through the years. Literature shows us what the history books often decline to show, - indeed often distort, intentionally cover up and even deny!

And in Ireland's case it is the suffocating power of the Catholic Church that is constantly being depicted through literature. The new Irish State established in 1922, where Irish and Catholic became synonymous! Where the dominance of the Catholic Church was undisputed! Where the long, multiple, encroaching tentacles of the Catholic Church extended into every aspect of life, - even into the carpark after the Sunday night dances!

This new Irish State where the new government was so anxious to prove to the English government that they could maintain a peaceful, moral society in Ireland and so justify their newly-granted independence. This new Irish State where the government was thus apparently only too willing to hand over responsibility for the overall education and the induction of moral standards, - establishing the moral fibre of the nation, - to religious orders of priests and nuns. Collusion between Church and State! And so the Irish nation became overwhelmingly imbued and subdued with the religious propaganda of the patriarchal, male-dominated Catholic Church.

Our social commentators, - those who have put pen to paper, - criticising, mocking and holding up for ridicule through satire, that which is folly and so hypocritical within society, pointing out that which most people do not even see through! And so we have the satirical TV series *'Father Ted'*; the iconic and bitter-sweet novels and dramas such as *'Tarry Flynn', 'Philadelphia Here I come!'* and of course James Joyce's *'The Dubliners'.* All showing the reality of life in 20th century Ireland. A harsh reality by any standards!

'Tarry Flynn', written by the Irish novelist and poet **Patrick Kavanagh** in 1948, is set in 1930s rural Ireland, in County Cavan. The novel depicts the life of a young farmer-poet, - Kavanagh himself, - and his search for identity and the meaning of life. The novel was banned by the Irish Censorship Board for being *'indecent and obscene'.* McQuaid again! McQuaid with a long finger in every pie! The ruling was overturned following a challenge by the publisher, although the novel did not return to publication until the 1960s. One of the most comical scenes is that depicted at mass on Sunday morning, with a captive audience, men seated at one side of the chapel and the women at the other, well separated. The result was that everybody was squint-eyed! Another scene depicts the Sunday night dance in the local hall, where again, men sat on one side and women on the other, and once the music started, there was a stampede across the floor to get a woman. Comical, yes, but also sad in the great sense of loneliness and isolation depicted within rural society, where all natural instincts were suffocated and smothered. And the banning of *'Tarry Flynn'* clearly showed the very close relationship between Church and State, politicians and Church authorities, fearful of the adverse effect that outside influences might have on Catholic morality. And so they combined and colluded to enforce a very vigorous opposition to liberal ideas and all works of art and literature that were considered at odds with Catholic values. Central to this policy was the passing of The Public Dance Halls Act in 1935 which regulated people's entertainment and which also included a prohibition on jazz music which was seen to be a bad influence on the Irish people. Reality of life in Catholic Ireland!

The 1937 Constitution, under the direction and guidance of McQuaid, had granted a special place to the Catholic Church in the life of the nation and recognised the role of women as mothers and home-makers. In his speeches and broadcasts, de Valera eulogised the role of women and painted an idealised picture of life in the Irish countryside. As one of the rural, Catholic poor, Patrick Kavanagh knew that the social realities of life for poor farming families was radically different to this utopian idyll of self-sufficiency and *'comely maidens dancing at the crossroads'*. In his poetry and in his fiction Kavanagh introduced his readers to male characters who were trapped by religion, by the land and by their mothers. When works such as his poem *'The Great Hunger'*, 1942 and his novel *'Tarry Flynn'*, 1948, were published, Kavanagh showed his increasing alienation from the Catholic Church and the artist in him was affronted by the official version of rural Ireland which was being sponsored by the government. As a consequence, *'Tarry Flynn'* was duly banned by the Irish Censorship Board, for being, in their words, *'indecent and obscene'* and it remained out of print until the 1960s. - A work that Kavanagh himself claimed was *'not only the best but the only authentic account of life as it was lived in Ireland this century.'*

The power of the Church in Ireland in a rural parish is well portrayed in the novel. Certainly Kavanagh's description of the parish priest as *'the centre of gravity'* could indeed be comical, if it were not so serious and so near the truth! Even the reading material available to Tarry is prescribed by the Church authorities, the standard work being the *'Messenger of the Sacred Heart'*. A missioner warns Tarry about reading the works of George Bernard Shaw, and his own mother warns him to attend the mission every evening, reminding him that when the Carlins failed to attend, their luck *'wasn't much the better of it.'* The priests set the moral tone of the parish and kept miscreants in check with uncompromising ferocity. They even presided over the parish entertainment and decided who was to be admitted and excluded. Like his neighbours, Tarry lives a life of unremitting drudgery. Reality of life in Catholic Ireland! *'Tarry Flynn'* tried in its own way to enlighten people at home and abroad about that reality, and as a result Kavanagh suffered the ultimate artistic sanction by having his novel banned.

In his poem *'The Great Hunger'*, Kavanagh is not referring to the Great Famine, with hunger for the potato, the staple diet of the Irish, but to the *'hunger'*, as in the desperate desire for sexual and spiritual freedom. In the poem, Patrick Maguire, an unmarried peasant, tied to his small acreage, is starved intellectually, psychologically, and spiritually as he struggles to eke out an existence. Maguire's present plight? *'Too long virgin'*. He regrets his unfulfilled promise to himself to marry, sighing, *'O God if I had been wiser!'*

The poem runs back through the sixty-five years of Maguire's existence, depicting his hopes, illusions, fears, as well as his personal, familial, and communal activities. And all against the stark background of his fourteen-hour day toiling through the growing season of the Irish potato from early spring seeding to October harvest. As the seasons pass and one potato crop follows the next, Kavanagh reveals Maguire's increasing awareness of the inexorable passing of time. Throughout, Maguire's aspirations for a fulfilling life clash with the reality of his thwarted existence. Reality of life in Catholic Ireland!

James Joyce in his collection of short stories, *'Dubliners'*, written in 1905, shows how the Catholic Church exercised a powerful, conservative influence over personal morality, family life and cultural and intellectual issues in Ireland. Joyce was convinced that the influence of the Catholic Church was negative, leading to a *'paralysis'*, a *'stagnation'*, a *'decay'* in personal and social life in Ireland, and his view is apparent in *'Dubliners'*, especially in the two stories *'The Sisters'* and *'Araby'*. Joyce describes the sense of decay, the *'odour of ashpit and old weeds and offal'* which *'hangs around'* all of his stories.

In the short story *'The Sisters'*, the young boy learns of the death of Fr. Flynn, an old priest whom he had visited regularly. He remembers his visits to the old priest, his shaky hands and snuff-smelling clothes, and some snippets of the Church doctrines he had taught him. But he is surprised by the great sense of freedom he now feels at the priest's death.

In the first paragraph, Joyce introduces graphically the *'paralysis'* that he sees affecting Dublin and its inhabitants. The boy is fascinated by the word *'paralysis'* which blights people's lives and stunts them spiritually, emotionally, and even physically. At the opening of this story, the paralysis of the priest is total, - he is dead.

The second theme Joyce introduces is that of *'simony'*. Joyce uses the notion of the sin of simony as a metaphor for the spiritual debasement of the Church. In this story the old priest has lost his faith and with it his priestly role. He is broken, physically, mentally and spiritually. His physical state, as described to the reader, betrays his spiritual state. His clothes are stained from the constant showers of snuff falling from his trembling hands. When he smiled he uncovered *'big, discoloured teeth and let his tongue lie upon his lower lip.'*

Paralysis itself, - the Church with its empty rituals, and rigid institutions, - is represented by a paralysed, broken priest. And with the priest's death, the boy experiences a sense of freedom, of release.

Joyce indicates in this story the power of what he saw as an empty religion in the friendship of the young boy with the old priest. There is no suggestion that the priest took any sexual interest in the boy, but the priest's physically decrepit state, a reflection of his spiritual decline, prompted the uncle and neighbour to exchange suggestive remarks about the priest's motives for his friendship with the boy.

In the short story *'Araby'*, the boy is incapable of a straightforward romantic approach to the girl. He has imbued the religious teaching and language from school and home, experiencing the loveless relationship of his uncle and aunt. Religion has permeated his consciousness so strongly that it is the only language of love he knows, and undermines his romantic and sexual instincts. Reality of life in Catholic Ireland!

'Philadelphia, Here I Come!' written by **Brian Friel** in 1964, is a tragicomedy, set in the fictional town of Ballybeg, County Donegal, portraying many themes central to life in 20th century Ireland. Centered on Gar's move to America, specifically Philadelphia, the play takes place on the night before and morning

of Gar's departure. Suffocating, mundane everyday lifestyle dominated by the Catholic Church teachings on morality, the intolerable isolation and loneliness, the inability of people to communicate any feelings of love, a nightly routine of the rosary, followed by the nightly visit from the parish priest, only here for his supper, failing to translate all this loneliness into some sort of meaning, and interested only in getting his annual holiday to Tenerife.

Gar sums up life in Ballybeg and his reasons for leaving:

'I've stuck around this hole far too long. I'm telling you, it's a bloody quagmire, a backwater, a dead-end! And everybody in it goes crazy sooner or later! Everybody!'

Emigration numbers soared. Young people leaving Ireland, never to return. Ireland being drained of its greatest asset, its young people. Just like Gar in Friel's play and in John B. Keane's *'Many Young Men of Twenty Said Goodbye'*. Saying goodbye, turning their backs on an economically depressed country, an agricultural economy crippled by tariffs and dependent on Britain for exports. All thanks to McQuaid and de Valera!

It was not just Ballybeg to which Gar was referring! - Reality of life in Catholic Ireland!

And portraying that reality rather than the myth of life in Catholic Ireland, was also the commitment of Kerry novelist, dramatist and short story writer **Bryan MacMahon**. In his works, MacMahon portrayed many of the themes which he saw as suffocating Irish life, such as fear of death with the Catholic Church teachings on hell, judgement and eternal damnation, on social ostracisation, and sexual love as a source of shame, guilt and disgrace, - again as a result of the Catholic Church teachings. Like his mother, MacMahon was a school teacher, and he always saw education as a liberation.

In his writings, and as he travelled around the country, MacMahon described his Ireland as a society in which fear of sin and punishment was widespread. He specifically referred to the Irish catechism, a question-and-answer road map for Irish catholics in the mid 20th century, and question 256, on page 62, *'What are the chief dangers to chastity?'*

And the answer?

'Idleness, *intemperance, bad companions, improper dances, immodest dress, company keeping and indecent conversation, books, plays and pictures*'.

A sexually repressed, guilt-ridden society, MacMahon recalling how they were constantly being chastised from the pulpit and told that it was a mortal sin to be in a lonely place with a girl! - Reality of life in Catholic Ireland!

And of course, we cannot leave out of this chapter **Edna O'Brien**! Just recently deceased and described by President Higgins as having *'the courage to confront Irish society'*.

In depicting the truth about life in Ireland through her early books - *'The Country Girls'* in 1960, *'Girl With Green Eyes'* in 1962, and *'Girls in Their Married Bliss'* in 1964, - O'Brien brought down on herself the wrath of a Catholic society, and gave her the reputation for scandal in her own homeland. In her novels, she spoke out about what until now had been kept under wraps in a staunchly Catholic Ireland, - female sexual desire and rebellion against parochialism and patriarchy. The authorities responded by banning her books, the clergy by denouncing her from the pulpit. In her home town of Tuamgraney, County Clare, which she described as *'not a town at all, but a hill with some pubs',* the people *'enclosed, fervid and bigoted'*, the local postmistress told her mother that, should her daughter dare to return, she *'should be kicked naked through the streets'*.

O'Brien got the sources for her books from her own young life, her suffocating childhood in an all-pervasive, male-dominated, stifling Catholic Church-controlled Irish society. Raised in a once-grand house, and the youngest child of a beleaguered mother and a sometimes tyrannical father, whom she described as *'too fond of the drink, but sadly for us, he was one of those unfortunate men who the drink did not agree with'*.

Again, in O'Brien's work we see the harsh reality of life in Ireland, and again, it is a reality very far removed from the hyped-up, idyllic images presented to the outside world! In reality, a sex-obsessed, Rome-directed, Jansenist-dominated Irish nation!

And McQuaid again! McQuaid and his vitriolic letters to Charlie Haughey, the then Minister of Culture. The books should not be allowed into any decent family! And he was banning them! But he first of all must have read them! In order to ban them! - Surely?

Kavanagh, Joyce, Friel, MacMahon and **O'Brien!** Just five of our literary greats who exposed the religious culture of the time, and a Catholic Church that depended for its very survival on thumping home a pessimistic view of God and salvation, a prudish emphasis on subduing the passions of the flesh, and an unhealthy focus on sin and sinning. Highlighting the repressive, suffocating, paralysing power of the Catholic Church in Ireland in the 20th century! And they suffered for it! More recently, - and how times have changed! - we have seen the likes of Magdalene survivors such as Christine Buckley, now deceased, Mary Murphy the mother of Bishop Casey's son, and Catherine Corless who exposed the Tuam Baby scandal, all being interviewed live on RTE's '*Late Late Show*'. All telling their stories on a public nation-wide platform! Who would have thought it would ever have been possible?

It's all there! All there in our literature! Life in mid-20th century Ireland! Suffocation, stagnation and sexual repression! And the result of this suffocation, stagnation and sexual repression in society?   - Enforced emigration! With over 400,000 people leaving independent Ireland, between 1951 and 1961, nearly a sixth of the total population recorded in 1951. They left because they had no other choice! And they left on a one-way ticket! They would not be coming back! The 1950s aptly referred to by historians as '*Ireland's lost decade.*'

And so the boats went out carrying Irish people away from their native shores. Oppression and suppression in a conservative, hierarchal society; lack of jobs;

economic poverty in a stagnant economy; the backwardness of the country; women who had been incarcerated in Magdalene and institutional establishments because of rape, incest, clerical sexual abuse, ashamed to remain; children given up for adoption and now untraceable; an Ireland held back from progress by de Valera's unrealistic image of healthy young people happy with life in an idyllic pastoral setting; intellectual isolationism, brought about by the various censorship boards of films and books, which closed Ireland off from the rest of the world, - the aim of McQuaid and de Valera being to keep Ireland pure and uncontaminated from outside, foreign influences.

So they left! They left in droves! They left to escape the poverty, the suffocation, the stifling, the repression of Irish life. De Valera's Ireland was not a welfare state as in England and other parts of Europe. So there was no assistance offered to overcome the dire, unmitigating poverty.

But change was coming! As we will see in chapter 7, *'The winds of change begin to blow'*.

So we have looked at the image of Ireland projected onto the world stage in the late 19th century and early-to-mid 20th century by the Irish Tourism agencies, by de Valera and his Fianna Fail government in the newly independent Irish Free State, and his *'holy alliance'* with John Charles McQuaid, the highest ecclesiastical authority in the country, - and then we looked at the contrasting reality! Fast forward now to today!

On the evening of 15th February 2024, the Irish-Belgian drama *'Small Things Like These'* premiered at the 74th Berlin International Film Festival.

'Small Things Like These' is a historical drama film about intergenerational trauma and the Magdalene Laundries scandal. Written by Enda Walsh, based on the 2021 novel of the same name by Claire Keegan, directed by Tim Maliant and starring Cillian Murphy, the film is set in New Ross, County Wexford, in 1985.

The action focuses on the main character, Bill Furlong, played by Cillian Murphy, a coal merchant and family man in the busiest part of the year, the weeks leading up to Christmas. While delivering an order of coal to his local convent one morning, Bill comes across something that causes him to confront his past and question the role that the Church plays in his society.

The film has been reviewed by the Guardian newspaper as a '*piercingly painful Magdalene Laundries drama*', with Murphy witnessing '*Ireland's church's abusive workhouses for unwed mothers in an absorbing Dickensian story based on recent history.*'

Cillian Murphy himself calls Ireland's Magdalene Laundries scandal a '*collective trauma*'.

And the Guardian continues:

'*Delivering coal to the church laundry – a place from which locals avert their eyes, as if from Dracula's castle – he walks straight in and sees the terrified girls for himself, like abused serfs. Each of them, he realises, resembles his own poor unmarried mother, who would assuredly have ended up in a place like this had she not been taken in by a wealthy local woman. The church sister – a dead-eyed performance of cool bureaucratic tyranny from Emily Watson – is icily aware that Bill is now in possession of a secret that could damage her and that, as a man, his (possible) objection would carry far more weight than one from the town's women. But she has his daughters' educational future in her hands.*

There is something very Dickensian in this story, signalled by Bill's boyhood ownership of David Copperfield, though with a fierce pessimism and anger that Dickens might not have favoured. And the ending is deeply strange; is it actually happening or not? I was so rapt, so caught up in this film, that I wasn't aware that it was going to be the ending until the screen faded to black. It is an absorbing, committed drama.'

Cillian Murphy himself spoke about '*the oppressive power of Catholicism, Irish-*

style', and the *'complicity, silence and shame,'* evident now in *'a dysfunctional Christian society'.*

And all exposed on the world stage! Shattering forever the last lingering vestiges of an idyllic Irish Catholic society!

All of Murphy's words must surely sum up our Irish nation as a society in the 20th Century! An Ireland suppressed and repressed by the overwhelming, suffocating and paralysing grip of the Catholic Church, - Irish-style! The combination of State and Church and the collusion between the two that was peculiar to Ireland, - it was precisely this that made Irish society what it became in the 20th century.

A society where priests and nuns were revered and respected, almost adored! Practically bowed down to and genuflected to in the street! The local priest who reigned supreme, - dictating people's lives, how they lived; how they thought; their health, - with abortion and birth control forbidden under pain of sin, resulting in large families and the accompanying poverty and struggle for survival in an economically depressed country; even their diet, with various days of fast and abstinence and what food could be eaten on certain days. A society where permission from the parish priest was needed for any woman who needed a hysterectomy, for example, or any other treatment for any *'feminine'* issue. A society were the long tentacles of the Church stretched everywhere, into each and every aspect of people's lives, - even into the car-park after the Sunday night dances - the dance itself of course run by the local priest!

So! Three completely different scenarios presented to the world, portraying life in Ireland in the 20th century.

We have the idyllic image put out by the various Tourist Boards, depicting Ireland as the land of one hundred thousand welcomes, a friendly and welcoming people, a place to recharge the spiritual batteries, amongst the enchanting scenery, the secluded beaches, the solitary places to be found in valleys, hills and dales, forests and mountains, and of course, the ancient spiritual sites of our pagan and Celtic ancestors. The Ireland of St. Patrick! And all in the attempt to sell Ireland to the tourist! A particular image of St. Patrick used and manipulated for a particular agenda! In just the same way as the Catholic Church used and manipulated a particular image of Mary Magdalene for their own agenda in the Magdalene institutions!

And we have the equally idyllic scenario presented by de Valera. A pure nation, a highly moral nation, a nation uncontaminated by western or other worldly influences. A pure nation, where the family unit was paramount! Where people were happy in the simple, '*frugal*' ways of life. A religious land, where people lived in the '*faith of our fathers*'. - A wholly unattainable vision!

The entire hypocrisy of it all!

The hypocrisy of Eamon de Valera, the upholder and promoter of the family as a sacred unit, the advocate of women as mothers and wives, - and himself the son of an unmarried mother! Self-proclaimed as the father figure, the patriarch of Irish society, - and himself not even Irish, - but American! And sent off to Ireland by his mother when he was just two years old! So, in reality, the man who had a fervent regard for the role of mothers in the home and within the family unit, and a strong belief in marriage as a fundamental unit of society, had experienced neither of these in his early years. Éamon de Valera, a prominent figure in Irish history, who grappled with questions surrounding his own parentage and legitimacy, as any search on the internet will tell you.

And then we have the picture of Ireland portrayed by our literary greats! What a difference!

What a difference between the image and the reality!

Chapter 4:

'Bless me Father'! Being a good Catholic - Irish-style!

What exactly constituted being a *'good Catholic'* in mid-20th century Ireland? I was in primary school in the late 1950s and early 1960s, in the Presentation Convent in Portadown. So I know what being a good Catholic meant back then! And how could I not know? It was drummed and beaten into us at school by nuns, on a daily basis! The 1950s! That decade often referred to by historians as Ireland's *'lost decade'*.

And not just *'being a good catholic'* but *'being seen'* to be a good Catholic! That was very important!

It was all about religion in those days, all about being holy, whatever that actually meant! Nothing about Spirituality. And there is a difference! A huge difference!

Religion is merely a label, a name, a brand, and has been used throughout history as a means to many ends. Religion is a divisive force, not a unifying one. Wars have been fought over religious affiliations, families have been split, murders and atrocities committed, too terrible for the ear. And all in the name of religion. Adherence to a particular religion has unleashed unimaginable extremes in violence. Countries have been conquered in the name of religion. Religion has been used to incite hatred, murder and revenge. And religion can be instilled into one any of us, at any stage in our life, manipulating us, controlling us, intimidating us, depending on the various techniques used.

Spirituality, on the other hand, transcends all religions. Spirituality cannot be instilled into us by any external force. Spirituality is our own individual connection to Spirit, and each one of us must find that connection for ourselves. We cannot inherit that connection from our parents or ancestors -

unlike religion. Spirituality is the inner knowing that there is a much greater force than us at work in the universe, and in our daily lives. Spirituality is not a show, a display, a flamboyance. Spirituality does not seek approval or recognition in outward displays of prayers or religious rituals. And Spirituality is an understanding and an acceptance that we are all of Divine Essence, and we are all one, in the totality of All That Is.

Spirituality allows your soul to fly freely, unfettered and unchained, released from the cage of enclosed thinking, from the confines of absolutism, from the dictates of those who profess to know what is best for you, what is best for your immortal, unique soul, and from the control and manipulation of those who claim to have all the answers.

And all of this is what being a good Catholic is most certainly NOT about!

Religion means bondage, Spirituality means freedom! And growing up a good Catholic in the mid 20th century meant you were imbued with the religious dogmas and teachings of the Catholic Church, and you conformed and adhered to those dictating rules and regulations!

Being a good Catholic and being seen to be a good Catholic back then meant going to mass on Sunday and to confessions at least once a month; regular attendance at various devotions and benediction; doing the stations of the cross; devotion to Mary and the various saints; receiving the sacraments; learning the catechism; attending the Lenten services; attending the missions during Lent, - given by members of religious orders such as the Carmelites, the Redemptrists or the Passionanists, - and which were always full of theatrical entertainment as the missioners shouted and thumped their way through their sermons; observing Church-designated days of fast and abstinence; not working on Sundays; attending Sunday school, - the further instilling of Catholic Church propaganda for a few hours on Sunday afternoons; observing the first Friday of every month as a day of special devotion to the Sacred Heart, - in the belief that those who went to mass and received Holy Communion on nine consecutive first Fridays would receive the grace of final repentance, - according to Margaret Mary Alocoque who claimed to have been told this in one of her visions; filling your Lenten box for Trocaire; paying your dues to the clergy; paying for masses to be said for various requests; buying novenas of masses; having pictures of the Sacred Heart or the Child of Prague on the mantelpiece or the dresser, - the Child of Prague being a particular object of devotion as it was believed to bring good luck; visiting various religious sites; money offerings at funerals; contributing to the missionaries and raising funds for them; contributing money for the '*black babies in Africa*'; donating to the Church coffers; suffering through penance for your sins; nightly family rosary, followed by a litany of an impressible variety of saints, and the recitation of the Virgin Mary's numerous titles, - Mary Queen of Virgins, Star of the Sea, Queen of Heaven, Refuge of Sinners, Queen of Peace, Queen of Angels, Mother of God etc.; wearing a miraculous medal; blessing yourself with holy water; making the sign of the cross when you passed a church; gaining indulgences to wipe away all your sins, and hence get straight into heaven; being an altar boy or later, an altar girl; attending a Catholic school; getting married in a Catholic church; going on pilgrimage to the likes of St. Patrick's Purgatory Lough Derg, Knock or Lourdes; taking part in the Corpus Christi processions, and the processions during May where we crowned Our Lady, - May being the special month of devotion to Mary; getting our throats blessed on 3rd February, the feast day of St. Blaise, patron saint of sore throats. And, - very important! No sex outside of marriage! - Sure we didn't even know what sex was!

So between one thing and another, we were always very busy! Kept very busy being good Catholics! This was full-time!

And then of course, there was the non-questioning of any Catholic Church rule, regulation or dogma; the bowing down, subservience and deference demanded by the clergy; the genuflecting, right to the ground in front of the altar; having a priest or nun in the family, - that was the '*wow*' factor!

And a good Catholic priest? A good Catholic priest was one who kept tags on his parishioners and kept them all in line; who knew all about them; who visited the homes; administered the sacraments; persuaded old people in hospitals and retirement homes to leave their money and estate to the Church; took in money for Church repairs, building projects etc., and of course, who shouted loudly from the pulpit! Hell, fire and brimstone and eternal damnation!

And so we doffed our hats and side-stepped off the pavement when we met a priest or nun. We doffed our hats again and blessed ourselves when we passed a church. And we blessed ourselves again and genuflected every time we passed the altar rails. And we drenched ourselves and each other in holy water, - tap water especially blessed by the priest. And we greeted and parted with those immortal words instilled into our brains - *'God bless!'*

Yes! We were all good Catholics in mid 20th century Ireland! The very best Catholics in the world, some might say!

Because we knew that being a good Catholic helped greatly in getting an education, getting a job or promotion, respectability in society and the opening of all sorts of doors. So we were initiated into the various stages of life, given our rites of passage, through the seven sacraments of the Catholic Church - from the cradle to the grave, from Baptism through to Extreme Unction at the point of death.

Collecting social capital! That's what we were doing! We just played along in the game!

That meant obeying the rules in all areas, doing what we were told, not questioning, keeping our heads down. And going to mass every Sunday! And confessions! *'Bless me father......'*

'Bless me Father for I have sinned .... I have said the Confiteor, Father....It is one month since my last confession Father. Father, I ....'

And then we proceeded to make up some sins, - sure we had to! Always being told we were sinners and going to hell if we didn't confess, we had to make up something! So that's what we did! We made it up! We lied! And then the priest gave us penance to do for doing something we had never done!

And we continued to pray to St. Anthony when we lost something, to St. Christopher for a safe journey, to St. Jude for success in exams, - he was the patron saint of hopeless cases after all! And then St. Martin - he was a good all-rounder, - he could make anything happen! And we continued lighting candles for success in exams, or when we wanted anything. - Which was always!

This was our world! We knew no other! A world of bleak and bland religion, a harsh and authoritarian regime that filled us with guilt and fear. Fear of God, fear of the Devil and all his wicked angels, fear of hell and fear of eternal damnation.

So we struggled through this *'vale of tears, mourning and weeping'*, - with our bleak view of human nature, - imploring, requesting, beseeching, begging, praying to an external God, a big man with a beard somewhere up beyond the clouds - a being who never existed!

We *'kept the faith'.* And the faith kept us! The *'faith of our fathers'.* We blindly obeyed. And what does blind faith do? - It makes fools of us all!

Chapter 5:

The long tentacles of the Catholic Church in 20th-century Ireland

Growing up in Ireland in the mid-20th century meant that every aspect of one's life was dominated and dictated by the Catholic Church. Like a hugh encroaching octopus, it had tentacles everywhere! Education, healthcare and social services - all under the control of the Catholic Church, even though the State public purse funded it all!

The Catholic Church dictated our year, even more so than did the changing seasons. Both our school and home routines and activities were structured around the religious calendar, school and home being where we learned to obey, without questioning, the authority of the Church and adhere to its rules and regulations. And where we learned the Catechism, - known as *'McQuaid's Catechism'* for obvious reasons, - a book of questions and answers which had to be learned off by heart. First question: *'Who is God?'* And the answer? *'God is our father who lives in heaven.'* And woe betide anyone who got a Catechism answer wrong when the priest came in! Or even stumbled over the answer! You could be held back from First Communion or Confirmation for that! And not only that, but you were sure to get a wallop from the nun when the priest left!

Baptism at birth, - that got us into this Catholic club, - and without being baptised we would never get into heaven! Nor even into a local school! Baptism made us a Catholic! It put a stamp, an identifying mark on us! And only Catholics got past those pearly gates and into heaven. No Protestants! Simply because the Catholic religion was the one and only true religion. And a still-born baby or a baby who died before being baptised would go to a special place called *'Limbo'*, because that baby still had the stain of original sin on its soul, and therefore did not qualify for heaven. *'Limbo'* was not like hell, though, as there was no fire or flames, but that baby would never see God. - So we were told!

First Confession, First Communion and Confirmation, - these were the sacraments into which we were initiated in our early growing-up years. Very important! Confirmation so important that the bishop himself came to perform the ceremony!

Mass and Holy Communion every Sunday, - non-negotiable! And in order to receive Communion, the body of Christ, we had to be fasting from the evening before. Friday was fish day, no meat allowed. Then we had the various days of both fast and abstinence, - such as Ash Wednesday and Good Friday, - days when we were allowed only one main meal and two collations, again, with no meat. Lent was an ongoing time of penance and deprivation, lasting about seven weeks, and demanded such practices as giving up sweets and donating our precious pennies to the Lenten Trocaire box.

Then there were the Ten Commandments! Also to be learned off by heart! We understood the ones about not stealing, killing or telling lies. They were easy to get your head around. But *'Thou shalt not covet thy neighbour's wife'* or *'I am the Lord thy God, thou shalt not have strange Gods before me'*. What did all that mean? We never asked, - we just learned it all off by heart.

We were brought up with an unhealthy obsession with sin and sinning! Both *'mortal'* and *'venial'*. The mortal sins were the worst. They could get you put down into hell if you died with one of those black marks on your soul. Venial sins were not just so bad. They could be wiped away by various forms of prayer and penance, such as plenary indulgences. By some sort of magic wave of the wand, these plenary indulgences wiped away all the stains from your soul, leaving you with a clean slate! Confession too left you with a clean slate, after you recited whatever prayers the priest gave you for your penance. The more serious your sin, the more penance you got! We were always told we were sinners! Always reminded that God was watching every move, knew every thought, always judging, always punishing, always waiting for us to stumble and then, - pounce!

And as we grew older, we had more rules and regulations! Now, as young adults, we felt more of the Catholic Church oppression seeping into even more areas of our lives. We had reached adulthood, but we were still stifled and suppressed. Still dictated to. What we could do, but mostly what we could not do. No one could attend the Protestant Trinity College without permission from the parish priest. That was right up until 1968. No one could get married in any church except a Catholic church and the ceremony performed by a Catholic priest . And no woman could have any medical *'female'* procedure done without permission from that same parish priest. A new mother had to be *'churched',* - a ritual performed after Sunday morning mass, at the altar rails, in front of everyone. The new mother needed to be *'cleansed'*, blessed by the priest because she had defiled her body by pregnancy and child-birth.

As adults, we now had to contribute to the upkeep of the clergy, by paying dues in the weekly collection envelope, each parishioner identified by the number on the envelope. And shamed into it by the humiliating public announcement at a particular Sunday Mass every year as to how much each and every parishioner contributed, starting with the highest, and so on down to the lowest. Shame and guilt! Powerful weapons! Further shame and guilt attached to offerings at funerals, money which was reputed to be given to the priest for masses to be said for the departed soul, to get that soul into heaven. Peter's Pence was another due to be paid, this one towards the upkeep of the pope in Rome. And then there were demands for contributions for repairs to any church buildings, with the reward of having your name inscribed on a pew in the church, so everyone knew about it, and again, guilt if you hadn't. To get your name on a stained glass window cost more, of course. Always looking for money! From birth to the grave! This was certainly an expensive club! The collection box at Sunday Mass was passed around not just once but twice! First for the weekly envelopes for the *'support of our pastors'* and then round it always came again for some other purpose!

And the Walls Came Tumbling Down!

Religious fervour, instilled into us, was almost fanatical. The Virgin Mary, the Mother of God, was held up to us as the epitome of holines, the role model for young girls. May was the month especially devoted to her, and we made May altars in her honour, with special hymns, ceremonies and processions throughout the month. The rosary was especially in honour of Mary as well, recited every evening in every Catholic home, kneeling on the floor. And of course, every family had someone named Mary!

We were never taught about sex or sexuality. Sex and pregnancy were the exclusive domain of the married couple. The physical aspect of sexuality was deemed disgusting and sinful. And the powerful emotions that naturally emerge during adolescence? Never ever spoken about! All kept secret!

Church festivals and holy days, sacraments, weekly mass and confession, devotions, stations of the cross, novenas, benediction, first Fridays. These all punctuated our year and our daily life. There was no time for anything else! Every minute of our day, our week, our month, our year, was controlled and dictated by the Catholic Church.

Even the most private and intimate! Contraception, abortion, divorce - all strictly forbidden. Mixed marriage also forbidden, and any child of such a union had to be brought up in the Catholic faith. And if any person did separate from their marriage partner, then they were denied access to Holy Communion. No divorce, no birth control! - No anything that was not *'acceptable to the Ecclesiastical Authorities'*!

Then there was the paying for indulgences, and for masses and various novenas to be said for those who had passed, the compulsory paying of dues for the upkeep of the clergy, the pilgrimages to various religious sites, - it went on and on. And over it all hung the fear, the fear instilled at an early age, the fear of hell and damnation, and of course the shame and guilt! A fear strengthened each year with the annual *'Missions'* during Holy Week! Thunder and lightening blasting from the pulpit! The fear of a punishing God, fear of Hell, fear of Purgatory and even fear of Limbo for those children who were still-born or died without being baptised! And the twisted fear of sex! - That most abhorrent of crimes!

Suffering and pain were the way to God! Penance had to be done for any '*sin*' committed! And the greatest '*sin*', needing the greatest of penance and atonement was pregnancy outside of marriage! But only for the woman! Ironic indeed, when so many priests and Church hierarchy were '*enjoying the pleasures*' of the '*sins of the flesh*'! Only we did not know about any of that back then!

An education system completely in the control of the Catholic Church! Propaganda and brainwashing! Appointment and dismissal of teachers! Appointment and dismissal of anyone, in any walk of life, who disputed or questioned the Catholic Church or its dogmas and teachings in any way!

The priest, on his regular round of visitations, arriving unannounced at your door meant you had to leave whatever it was you might be doing, - preparing food, up to your elbows in soap suds, down on your knees scrubbing, or changing the baby's nappy, - none of that mattered right now! The priest was here, he had to be attended to, and the best china was taken out. And during the missions in Lent, two or three missionaries might arrive unannounced, along with the local priest. And all had to be offered tea!

The long tentacles of the Catholic Church in 20th century Ireland! Encroaching into every aspect of life! Dominating, controlling, intimidating! Dictating even what we were allowed to read! Intellectual isolationism instigated by de Valera and McQuaid as part of their social engineering policy, with strict censorship in books and films, meant that we were sealed off from the rest of the world. Sermons thundered out from the pulpit warned continuously and relentlessly about the extreme dangers to our faith and morals posed by uncensored literature and films, immodest dress, excessive drinking and the increasing desire for pleasure, materialism and secularism.

Comics to which we did have access included the '*Bunty*' and '*Judy*', with the enthralling adventures of the *'Four Marys'*, - four boarding school friends all called Mary, with their stories of secret midnight feasts and orphan girls overcoming enormous difficulties, - and the *'Beano'* and *'Dandy'* with Dennis the Menace and his dog Gnasher, Minnie the Minx, Desperate Dan, Roger the Dodger and Beryl the Peril, amongst others.

Television opened us up to the mesmerising worlds of *'Andy Pandy'*, the *'Woodentops'*, *'Bill and Ben the Flower-Pot Men'* and others such as *'Romper Room'*, *'Blue Peter'*, *'Postman Pat'*, *'Watch with Mother'*, *"The Waltons'* - with John-Boy.

Then we had Billy Bunter, Olive and Popeye, Laurel and Hardy, Punch and Judy, Sooty and Sweep, Tom and Gerry, the Flintstones. Such innocence! And of course, *'The Lone Ranger' and 'Dr. Who'*. And RTE gave us such as *'Crackerjack'* with Eamon Andrews and *'The School Around the Corner'*. All far removed indeed from *'Mrs. Brown's Boys'*! Or *'Father Ted'*!

The newspapers we were permitted to read included the *'Irish Press'* and the *'Irish Independent'*, with the more up-market Protestant *'Irish Times'* reserved for the more intellectual. Newspapers and magazines from *'across the water'* were denounced from the pulpit as being too scandalous for our pure minds, not for us to be reading, with their stories of divorce, family scandals, murders, political and public affairs. And we were forbidden to read the *'stars'* section! - Fortune telling! That was a mortal sin! No Mystic Megs! No Psychic Salleys! We were confined to reading *'Our Boys'* produced by the Christian Brothers, which consisted of stories about Irish *'heroes'* such as Robert Emmet or Padraig Pearse, and battles such as the 1798 rebellion or 1916; *'Ireland's Own'* and *'Ireland's Eye'*. And then the weekly *'Irish Catholic'* and the *'Messenger of the Sacred Heart'*. Reading all about the lives of the saints and martyrs, miracles at Lourdes, Fatima, Knock, details about the next pilgrimage, about charity work. And of course not forgetting, the weekly parish bulletin! The weekly parish bulletin that told us all we needed to know!

The greatest wonder and mystery is, how did we ever allow ourselves to be in that position? How did we just accept what was imposed on us without questioning any of it? How did we not see all that superstition on which Catholicism was based? Why did we not try to assert our own sovereignty? Why did all those big strong lads cowering under a brutal Christian Brother with a cane in his hand not fight back? There were more boys than there were Brothers! They certainly had the advantage of numbers!

And the answer? - Fear! Fear of what the Catholic Church could do to you! No one wanted to rock the boat, and without support and back-up, you were on a suicide mission! - Holy annihilation!

None of us chose to be Catholic! We were born into it! And we were reared in it! We were conditioned! Conditioned through fear! Catholic beliefs, teachings and dogmas drummed into us from a very early age, even before we could walk! And our days growing up were filled with Catholic rituals, our whole year based around the Catholic Church services. School, the home, the work place, - the Catholic Church dominated it all. An impregnable wall of steel! Church tentacles everywhere! And fighting against it was useless! You couldn't win! And not only could you not win, but by even questioning any of it, you could be destroyed. Your career, your social standing, - all could be destroyed - at one swoop of the Catholic Church fangs!

Collusion between church, state and parents! Parents backed the nuns and priests to the hilt! Not realising that they too were victims of Catholic Church propaganda! Conditioned from birth! In their eyes, the nuns could do no wrong! There was only one person whose words could top that of the nuns! And that was the priest!

The control the Catholic Church exerted over people's lives in 20th century Ireland was complete, total and absolute! Its long tentacles infiltrating, permeating, oozing into every corner! Even into the bedroom!

Chapter 6:

The winds of change begin to blow

Everything changes! That is the nature of life! And that is because everything, absolutely everything, - including ourselves - is energy! And energy is in a constant flux of change.

Indeed we could well say the only constant thing is change! Paradoxical or what? And the most timeless song that can be written is therefore one about that very fact! Bob Dylan knew it! Hence his classic, '*The Times They Are a-Changin'*.

And when was it written? In 1963! Right in the middle of McQuaid's reign! The song was a protest anthem and a call to action.

By the 1960s, Irish society was surely changing. On the slow burner yes, but there was a gradual growing awareness and intolerance of the bleakness, the dullness, the stagnation of life in rural Ireland, a growing questioning of old, obsolete values, and a growing desire that Ireland come into the 20th century with other countries. The process of the unravelling of the whole web of traditional Irish Catholicism had begun and was gathering momentum, - a process that was both unstoppable and irreversible!

The lines of Dylan's song underscored the transformative nature of society, the changing social climate, and the need to adapt to it:

'*The present now will later be past. / The order is rapidly fadin'.........../ And you better start swimmin' or you'll sink like a stone ..../ For the times, they are a-changin'*...............

Come writers and critics who prophesize with your pen / And keep your eyes wide, the chance won't come again / And don't speak too soon, for the wheel's still in spin / And there's no tellin' who that it's namin' / For the loser now will be later to win / For the times, they are a-changin'............

Come senators, congressmen, please heed the call / Don't stand in the doorway, don't block up the hall / For he that gets hurt will be he who has stalled / The battle outside ragin' / Will soon shake your windows and rattle your walls / For the times, they are a-changin'.............

Come mothers and fathers throughout the land / And don't criticize what you can't understand / Your sons and your daughters are beyond your command / Your old road is rapidly agin' / Please get out of the new one if you can't lend your hand / For the times, they are a-changin'.

An era of change ushered in, - an era of change which the Catholic Church in Ireland tried desperately to stall. To hold onto their conservative, authoritarian, orthodox Church teachings and dogmas, unable to fully grasp that *'Your sons and your daughters are beyond your command',* as a whole new world began to emerge, a world where very soon, McQuaid and de Valera would no longer have control, where all they built up would tumble down around them!

We have considered earlier in this book the reasons for the two papal visits to Ireland - that of Pope John Paul II in September 1979, and Pope Frances in August 2018, and how each of these visits was an attempt by the Catholic hierarchy to stall the moral decline, to plug the hole in the dyke, to bolster up the conservative Catholic Church. And we saw there was a remarkable difference in the two visits! In both cases it was that impending *'moral decline',* already begun, that brought each pope here to our shores. We have considered too how Catholicism was once so all-pervading in Irish life that *'Irish'* and *'Catholic'* had become synonymous.

So, what happened? What happened to explain the fact that the same Catholic Church that had enjoyed unprecedented power and influence in Ireland, that same Catholic Church that had wielded so much power over people's lives in Ireland, was now, by the 1960s on the decline? And by the 1990s, and certainly by the early 21st century, that same Catholic Church had totally lost its grip? And it was not just in Ireland! The decline of the Catholic Church is a world-wide phenomenon, not just an Irish one! But in Ireland their control had permeated into every area of life, as we have seen. So how come they were not able to hold onto that power?

It is often said that the most critical, the most crucial, the most dangerous time for any institution or government is when it begins to change, to ease restrictions, to loosen the rope, to bring in some sort of reform, to adapt to a changing world. And the Second Vatican Council, 1962-1965 was an attempt to change how the Catholic Church interacted with an increasingly changing modern world. Changes were made, in an attempt to loosen Church regulations. Suddenly a lot of what we could NOT do under the threat of the pain of eternal damnation now became acceptable!

The First Vatican Council in 1870, had portrayed the Papacy as an absolute monarchy, emphasising the supremacy of the pope. Vatican II, under the direction of Pope John XXIII, now modified this, emphasising that the pope was now acting in line with his bishops, sharing responsibility and decision-making with them on matters pastoral and doctrinal. And emphasising that closer links should be made with other denominational Churches.

So a Catholic Church that in the previous century had condemned any form of religious liberty or non-orthodox thinking, now, in Vatican II, 1962-1965, committed itself to dialogue and interaction with all streams of religious thought and faiths, and more interaction with their own laity.

So how did the changes made in Vatican II affect the ordinary person going about his daily business? The teachings remained the same. But the rules and regulations changed in some ways.

The mass was now celebrated in English, or the language of the country, not in

Latin, with the priest facing the congregation, instead of with his back to them, now enabling the laity to participate for the first time.

Sunday mass was now changed to Saturday, if one preferred! Small consolation for those who had already passed and had a mortal sin on their soul if they had infringed against the strict and non-negotiable rule of attending Sunday mass!

The Body of Christ, the sacrament of Holy Communion, was now distributed to the laity in both the form of bread and wine, unlike previously, where the laity were offered only bread, the wine being reserved for the priest.

Now we could hold the Host in our hands, whereas before it was one of the worst sacrilegious crimes to touch it in any way. Even if dropped, it was only the priest who could pick it up. And people, members of the laity could now administer Holy Communion!

Women could now attend mass and church services without a head cover, unlike previously where a woman would not have dared to enter a church without such a covering!

Women could now wear trousers to such places as St. Patrick's Purgatory Lough Derg or climbing Croagh Patrick on pilgrimage in County Mayo. Not good news for the midgets!

Collective, or general confession was now suddenly available!

We were now allowed to work on Sundays, if necessary, and go to shops and markets.

Men and women were no longer required to sit in separate parts of the church.

And nuns' habits became shorter! Together with the head gear which was greatly reduced!

And the Walls Came Tumbling Down!

Just a few of the changes made by Vatican II. Just a few of the changes that the ordinary person saw as applying to him.

Poor McQuaid! His Grace was displeased! More participation of the laity in Church matters? Linking up ecumenically with the Protestant Church? Both absolutely unacceptable to McQuaid! McQuaid the anti-Protestant lobbyist! McQuaid, the anti-everything that was not Catholic!

But at 70 years of age and still without the *'red hat'*, he meekly acquiesced with the majority vote of the bishops and returned to Ireland. To continue with his old ways! The puppeteer pulling the strings! On his return, in a sermon in Dublin's Pro-Cathedral in Marlborough Street, he consoled his congregation:

'You may have been worried by much talk of changes to come. Allow me to reassure you. No change will worry the tranquility of your Christian lives......As the months will pass, gradually the Holy Father will instruct us how to put into effect the enactments of the Council. With complete loyalty as children of the one, true Church, we fully accept each and every decree of the Vatican Council.'

By showing himself as a dissident, by not obeying the rules laid out by *'he who must be obeyed'*, - the man at the very top of the Catholic Church pyramid, - McQuaid was on his way out! His star was falling!

And then came more bad news for him! A remote, hardline, pedantic and orthodox disciplinarian, determined to prevent what he saw as the break-up of the Catholic Church, McQuaid could do nothing to hold back the winds of change! Catholics could now go into protestant churches to take part in the services of baptism and the weddings of their protestant friends, - they could even act as bridesmaid or bestman! And they could attend protestant funerals. Mixed marriages were now permitted, and could be held openly during mass, in a catholic church.

And then some good news! Something for McQuaid to cheer about, something for him to applaud in a major press conference! Pope John XXIII was succeeded by Pope Paul VI, and in his 1968 '*Humane Vitae',* he banned contraceptives. McQuaid was ecstatic!

But then he learned that doctors in Dublin's first family planning clinic were ordering the contraceptive pill for medical reasons. McQuaid, now 75, but in good health, expected to carry on for a number of years. But he had stepped outside the pyramid! He had broken the pyramidal rules! He had gone against the highest in the pyramid! And in late December 1972 he was forced into retirement by those at the Vatican who saw him as a dissenting voice! Those in the Vatican who wanted to ease restrictions, who wanted closer ties and more communication with other denominations.

And then the '*Unmarried Mother's Allowance*' was introduced in January 1973, and even though the term '*illegitimate'* would not be abolished until 1987, there was already talk about addressing this and ensuring that children born outside of marriage would have equal succession rights. In 1990, the name was changed to '*Lone Parents Allowance'* and in 1997, to '*One Parent Family Payment.'*

And if this did not actually kill McQuaid, it certainly did not do his health any good! He died just a few months later, in April 1973 at Loughlinstown Hospital, still never having attained that elusive *'red hat'*.

With McQuaid dead, the winds of change were now blowing more strongly! And those winds of change gave rise to all sorts of scathing back-lashes!

In 1979, the British comedy '*Life of Brian'* hit the big screen. Acclaimed as the '*funniest movie ever made*', the film was a box office success, the fourth highest-grossing film in the United Kingdom in 1979, and highest-grossing of any British film in the United States that year. It has remained popular and has been named as the greatest comedy film of all time by several magazines and television networks, and it later received a 96% rating on '*Rotten Tomatoes*' with the consensus reading, *'One of the more cutting-edge films of the 1970s, this religious farce from the classic comedy troupe is as poignant as it is funny and satirical'.* In a 2006 Channel 4 poll, *'Life of Brian'* was ranked first on their list of the 50 Greatest Comedy Films.

The film's themes of religious satire were controversial at the time of its release, drawing accusations of blasphemy and protests from some religious groups. Thirty-nine local authorities in the United Kingdom imposed either an outright ban or an X - 18 years, - certificate. Some countries, including Ireland and Norway, banned its showing, and in a few of these, such as Italy, bans lasted over a decade. The filmmakers used the notoriety to promote the film, with posters in Sweden reading, *'So funny it was banned in Norway*!'

One of the Monty Python series, the film delivers a scathing, anarchic satire of both religion and Hollywood's depiction of all things biblical. The setting is Judea 33 AD, a time of poverty and chaos, with no shortage of messiahs, followers only too willing to believe in them, and exasperated Romans trying to impose some order in their conquered Jewish territories. Everyone and everything is mocked, - from ex-lepers, Pontius Pilate, the art of haggling, crazy prophets, Roman centurions, crucifixion, Mary Magdalene, Jesus himself.

The sluice gates were open! The Catholic Church was coming under scathing, satirical, cynical scrutiny world-wide.

George Carlin 1937-2008 was an American stand-up comedian, - one of the most famous of all time, - a social critic, activist and author. One of his most scathing comedic deliveries was on religion:

'Religion has convinced people that there is an invisible man living in the sky, watching everything you do, every minute of every day and the invisible man has a list of 10 specific things he does not want you to do. But if you do any of these things, he will send you to a special place of burning and fire and smoke and torture and anguish where you will live forever and suffer and burn and scream until the end of time. But he loves you! He loves you! He loves you and he needs money. He is all-present, all powerful, all knowing, all wise. Just can't

handle money! Religion takes in billions and billions of dollars, they pay no taxes, and somehow they always need money. You talk about a good BS story!'

And not to be outdone, Ireland made its own contribution!

'The Bishop and the Nightie'! A major milestone in challenging the power of the Catholic Church in Ireland! The first time a member of the Catholic Church hierarchy was made to look ridiculous in front of the public! Irish Catholic Church excessive and grossly exaggerated prudery exposed for what it was! - Farcical! Laughable! Silly!

In 1996, Gay Byrne on the *'Late Late Show'* asked a married woman guest, all in the light hearted fun and banter of a harmless fun quiz, what colour of nightdress she wore on her honeymoon night. When she replied that she could not remember, maybe not even wearing any at all, the Bishop of Clonfert, Dr. Thomas Ryan, denounced the entire episode from the pulpit in St. Brendan's Cathedral Loughrea, and reported his shock and utter disgust in a national Sunday newspaper. At first it appeared the public were in support of the bishop, but then the tide turned and the bishop found himself the object of laughter. It was indicated to RTE that Gay Byrne should be dismissed.

Gay was not dismissed, the public continued to laugh, and the *'Late Late Show'* continued as a national forum for topics of conversation, including priesthood, which had previously been regarded as *'don't go there'* territory. Bishop Eamon Casey and Father Michael Cleary were amongst the first of a line of high profile clerics on the *'Late Late Show',* - both to be later be disgraced for sexual abuse.

And then in 1995, Father Ted arrived in Ireland! *'Father Ted',* a sitcom created by Irish writers Graham Linehan and Arthur Mathews and produced by British production company Hat Trick Productions for British television channel Channel 4. It aired over three series from 21 April 1995 until 1 May 1998, including a Christmas special, for a total of 25 episodes. It aired on Nine Network for series 1 and ABC Television for series 2 and 3 in Australia, and on

And the Walls Came Tumbling Down!

TV2 in New Zealand. Popular or what?

This was far and away beyond what the Irish Catholic nation had ever been exposed to before! A caricature that portrayed priests as fools or intoxicated, debauched old scruffy drunks, and nuns as fawning, besotted women clinging onto every word of the priest, their entire life centered around mass and religious ceremonies, with a visit to or from the priest being a major event in their otherwise religion-infested lives.

A comedy that could not have been even imagined just a few decades earlier in *'Catholic Ireland'*. And guess what? The Irish nation loved it! *'Catholic Ireland'* exposed as a priest-ridden backwater, full of idiotic, imbecilic priests and fawning nuns, - and viewers laughed!

The late Dermot Morgan starred as the fictional Father Ted Crilly, who, together with Father Dougal McGuire, played by Ardal O'Hanlon, and Father Jack Hackett, played by Frank Kelly, were exiled, for various reasons, by Bishop Leonard Brennan, played by Jim Norton, to the equally fictional Craggy Island, a remote location off Ireland's west coast, where the three priests live together in the parochial house with their housekeeper Mrs. Doyle, played by Pauline McLynn.

Ted has supposedly been banished for alleged financial irregularities, after some money was found *'resting'* in his account, and a child was deprived of a trip to Lourdes so that Ted could go to Las Vegas; Dougal for an event only referred to as the *'Blackrock Incident'* which apparently left many nuns' lives irreparably damaged; and Jack for his alcoholism and womanising, particularly for an unspecified incident at a wedding in Athlone.

The show revolves around the priests' lives on Craggy Island, sometimes dealing with matters of the Church but more often dealing with Father Ted's schemes to either resolve a situation with the parish or other Craggy Island residents, or to win games of one-upmanship against his enemy, Father Dick Byrne of the nearby Rugged Island parish.

And like all satires, you do not actually need to know who or what is being satirised. The show is permeated with humour, each scene to be enjoyed for itself. But if you do know that it is the Catholic Church in Ireland, with its priests and nuns, that is being satirised and mocked, then the jokes are even funnier! And you will laugh the louder!

And as we are talking about satire, we cannot forget that iconic extended poem '*The Midnight Court*' written by Brian Merriman at the start of the 19th century. Satirical, scathing, sarcastic, bawdy and humorous, it is a direct attack on the conventions of the day, including the Catholic Church ruling on clerical celibacy:

'Another thing I'd like to mention, / That's beyond my comprehension – / Whatever made the Church create / A clergy that is celibate?'

And it has to be admitted! 'The *Midnight Court* ' could well be applied to Ireland in the 20th century! -

'Throughout the land may a new rule unfold / Of sexual freedom for young and for old..........'

And on a celibate priesthood:

'Most of these fellows, I truthfully believe, / Are lonely Adams asking God for an Eve / To be fair, it wouldn't do / To hang the lot because of the few / Sinking the ship wouldn't be the right plan, / Drowning the whole crew to get one man / Some have always been a right shower /Who are in the priesthood for the power / Tough old buzzards without any heart / Who think every woman is just a tart............ I've seen incontrovertible evidence that many a son / Could call a priest a father in more ways than one............In Ireland it has been demonstrably cruel / The damage that's done by this aimless rule. / The trouble, I assert, O Fount of Wisdom / Is that clerical celibacy is the bane of Christendom / And is nothing if not an abomination...........'

And thinking of this dramatic decline in the power of the Catholic Church in

And the Walls Came Tumbling Down!

Ireland reminds me of one of the most famous works of Percy Bysshe Shelly, 1792-1822, who is considered as one of the major English Romantic poets, and an important influence on subsequent generations of poets, including Robert Browning, Thomas Hardy, and W. B. Yeats.

In his poem *'Ozymandias',* Shelley deals with the theme of transience of power, as he describes the ruins of an ancient king's statue in a foreign desert. All that remains of the statue are *'two vast and trunkless legs of stone'* that *'stand in the desert',* and a head *'half sunk in sand'* along with a boastful inscription describing the ruler as the *'king of kings'* whose mighty achievements invoke awe and despair in all who behold them.

The inscription stands in ironic contrast to the decrepit reality of the statue, however, underscoring the ultimate transience of political power. The poem implicitly critiques such power through its suggestion that both great rulers and their kingdoms will fall to the sands of time.

The fact that even this *'king of kings'* lies decaying in a distant desert suggests that no amount of power can withstand the merciless and unceasing passage of time.

Ozymandias had believed that while he himself would die, he would leave a lasting and intimidating legacy through everything he built. Yet his words are ultimately empty, as everything he built has crumbled. The people and places he ruled over are gone, leaving only an abandoned desert whose *'lone and level sands'* imply that there's not even a trace of the kingdom's former glory to be found. The pedestal's claim that onlookers should despair at Ozymandias's works thus takes on a new and ironic meaning: one despairs not at Ozymandias's power, but at how powerless time and decay make everyone.

In the 1950s, in that *'lost decade',* the Catholic Church in Ireland, never a liberal institution by any standards, was largely ruled by a number of despotic and authoritative bishops who essentially belonged in a previous age, relics of a by-gone era, - notably Archbishop John Charles McQuaid of Dublin, whom we have already considered, Bishop Cornelius Lucey of Cork and Bishop Michael Browne of Galway. They were by no means the only such members of the ecclesiastical hierarchy at that time, but they were the strongest personalities among the clergy and clung to certain authoritarian, dictatorial, conservative attitudes, failing completely to read correctly the changing social mood and climate! And so they continued to attempt to rule the proverbial roost!

From the 1960s, a variety of factors combined to transform Irish society. From the premiership of Seán Lemass onwards, Lemass having succeeded de Valera, the State now prioritised economic growth over the more simple, orthodox, catholic nationalist vision of Irish society which had prevailed since independence and de Valera. Modernisation had brought the television to Ireland, and life was changed forever. There was no going back now to the isolationism of de Valera's vision. The country's first television network, Radio Telefis Eireann, received approval in 1960 after nearly a decade of debate that at one time involved the Vatican, because of the fear that the medium would corrupt the *'purity'* of the Irish culture. By 1980, over 90% of Irish households owned a television set, introducing international news and popular culture into living-rooms throughout the country and exposing Ireland to the rest of the world as never before. At the same time, the Catholic Church's influence on the Irish population diminished, helped on by programmes such as the *'Late Late Show'* first hosted by Gay Byrne, which facilitated the questioning of traditional structures of authority and society. Gay Byrne became the face of modern Ireland! And as has often been claimed - *'there was no sex in Ireland before television'*! Amended sometimes to *'there was no sex in Ireland before Gay Byrne'*!

But even before the clerical scandals broke into the public domain, the *'faith of our fathers'* was in decline, the *'we will be true to thee till death'* bit no longer appealing. As explained, the 1960s had started something unstoppable.

Diarmaid Ferriter, lecturer in history in St. Patrick's College, Dublin City

University, already referred to in a previous chapter, and now in his book *'Judging Dev'* published in 2007, makes the point that a new Ireland, a *'modern Ireland'*, could only emerge when de Valera was no longer Taoiseach, and in the largely merely ceremonial office of Irish President. Ferriter quotes from an Irish Times report, 25th September 2004, about how John Bruton, Fine Gael leader and Taoiseach 1994-1997 remarked that in the presidential election of 1966, when Tom O'Higgins came within so many votes of defeating de Valera, it marked a turning point away from *the 'dream of an Irish-speaking and self-sufficient Ireland towards a slightly more materialistic but more European destiny'*. (Diarmaid Ferriter, *'Judging Dev'* page 5)

And for Ferriter, the implication is clear:

'De Valera was standing in the way of modernisation; he was of no significance to a new generation, and the victory of 1966 was the faint sting of a dying, blind and irrelevant old wasp.' (Diarmaid Ferriter, *'Judging Dev'* page 5)

And Ferriter was not alone in his assessment! The poet Paul Durcan, as Ferriter points out, imagined him as an *'old, cranky kill-joy'* in his 1978 poem *'Making love outside Aras an Uachtarain',* and Neil Jordan used de Valera's funeral as the background to a short story which dealt with liberation from a suffocating past.

The same Eamon de Valera whom Tim Pat Coogan in his biography of de Valera in 1993, *'De Valera, long fellow, long shadow',* described as having done *'little that was useful and much that was harmful'*.

Once de Valera and McQuaid were gone, the expansion of the market and the influence of the media in subsequent decades ushered in a new Ireland, an Ireland based on more liberal and more individualist thinking, consumerism and materialism, the very things against which the Catholic Church had preached so vehemently for generations. The changing position of women was also crucial in modernising Ireland, particularly from the 1970s onward. Irish women challenged the patriarchal nature of Irish society and traditional

Church teaching on birth control and on the natural role of woman as mother and home-maker. The Irish mother had played a vital role in the development and transmission of Irish Catholicism from generation to generation. It was the mother who had gathered the family together for the nightly rosary, it was the mother who had fostered in the family a vocation to the religious, it was the mother who made sure the family attended mass and Catholic Church ceremonies and rituals. Now women had alternative sources of power through the work place and through public life. Women, a key pillar in bolstering up the Catholic Church in Ireland! That key pillar now gone! And the irony is not lost! Women! The key pillar in Irish Catholicism! Women, - against whom that same Catholic Church showed so much antaganism and animosity!

And then in the 1990s came the *'Celtic Tiger'*. Named in imitation of the so-called *'Asian Tiger'* economies in countries in the Far East. The *'Celtic Tiger'* needed skills and tradesmen, mechanical engineers, - all sorts of trained people to feed the growing momentum. The *'Celtic Tiger',* in effect a capitalist revolution, possible only because of various more progressive governments long divorced from de Valera's romantic image of an idyllic rural Ireland, governments that curbed government spending, brought in reforms in economic structures and introduced new fiscal measures - all rapidly transforming the Irish economy from an economy on the verge of bankruptcy in the mid 1980s, with the second highest rate of unemployment in Europe, into a booming, thriving capitalist economy, now praised as the fastest-growing economy in Europe.

The Irish nation now found itself dancing to a different tune! The rules had changed! The goalposts had moved! The younger generation of Irish now enjoyed the trappings and comforts of materialism and commercialisation far beyond what their parents before them had ever known. The Catholic Church preaching about *'holiness'* and *'poverty'*, the *'shallowness of money',* and de Valera's ideals of *'wholesome simplicity'* and *'frugal comforts'* now became obsolete, outmoded and outdated for this new generation of cash lovers! No one was listening! All caught up in the frenzy to make as much money as possible in as short a time as possible! The *'things of the spirit'* now had no chance against this new wealth and booming prosperity that was available to all!

The story of Ireland during the *'Celtic Tiger'* years is the story of the triumph of capitalism over Catholicism! And Catholicism had to recede first before capitalism could triumph! And why? Simply because, in a capitalist state, individualism is the key, and the Catholic Church did not believe in individualism. No! Theirs was a mindset of obedience and subservience, in an orthodox, unchanging society, and an orthodox, unchanging society is against the very principles on which capitalism is based. Free choice, free enterprise, free thinking, all inherent in a capitalist economy, had no place in a Catholic-Church-controlled Ireland. And so Catholicism lost out. Big time!

The most significant impact of the *'Celtic Tiger'* was the transformation of Ireland into a multi-ethnic country. The economic boom, with the increase of materialism, brought an increase in employment, and so began the influx of immigrants to feed this new employment demand. And with the increase in materialism, and the corresponding increase in employment, there came in turn a corresponding decline in religious vocations. And with the decline in religious vocations, came a corresponding decline in the Catholic Church power in education. And control of education so pivotal to their power!

Education! Education! Education! The power of education! Survey findings have indicated that the higher the level of educational attainment, the lower the level of orthodox religious belief and acceptance of Church teaching. And control of Irish education - its ethos, school management and teaching appointments - taken over from the British government in the nineteenth and early twentieth centuries, was regarded as essential if Catholic faith and values were to be passed down to future generations.

The Second Vatican Council, as we just saw, loosened Church regulations, and the 1960s marked the start of a long period of decreased vocations in the United States and Ireland from which the Church has not even yet recovered.

And without religious vocations, the Catholic Church in Ireland could not sustain itself. The schools, which were previously under the control of religious orders, and the chief propaganda mechanism for the Catholic Church in Ireland, were now slowly being handed over to independent, lay and state control. As were the hospitals. A notable example was the decision of the Sisters of Charity to leave health care in 2017.

The Celtic Tiger! It did not just happen suddenly by some miracle in the 1990s! The groundwork had already begun in the late 1960s. How? Through a recognition that the extension of educational opportunity was a central aspect of national economic development, and that *'Ireland needs to be catering for the new age of technology'*. These were the words of one man who was not afraid of McQuaid! Spoken in 1966 by Donogh O'Malley, Irish Education Minister, July 1966 to March 1968. The same Donogh O'Malley who described the Irish education system as *'a dark stain on the national conscience'*. The education system established by McQuaid and de Valera! The education system whereby a third of children who finished primary school dropped out of secondary education by the age of fourteen years, simply because parents of large families were unable to pay the fees. So that meant that one third of the potential work force in Ireland were unskilled. And unskilled workers, as O'Malley understood, were not much use in the coming new age of technology!

In Northern Ireland, the situation was very different! As part of Great Britain, education in Northern Ireland was already free for all. When I started in University College Dublin in 1968, full grants for both tuition and living expenses were available to all, regardless of the financial situation of parents. I worked in Boston during the summer months, as did hundreds of other Irish university students. The difference was that I was able to use my earnings to travel before I came back to college, whereas the Irish students had to save every single dollar for their university fees, as there was nothing in the way of grants available to them.

And it was this same better state provision of education and healthcare, and not just employment opportunities, that brought emigrants in boat loads from Ireland to neighbouring United Kingdom! Social change in Ireland and policies intending to correct this deficit were often met with strong resistance, as we saw previously, such as Noël Browne's proposed Mother and Child Scheme. As a former Health Minister, O'Malley had first-hand experience of running the department which had attempted to introduce this scheme and understood the processes that caused it to fail, such as resistance from Department of Finance and John Charles McQuaid. And it was this that influenced O'Malley's strategy in presenting the free-education proposal.

As Minister for Education, it was O'Malley who extended the school transport scheme and commissioned the building of new non-denominational comprehensive and community schools in areas where they were needed. He introduced Regional Technical Colleges (RTCs), now called Institutes of Technology, in areas where there was no third level college. The best example of this policy is the University of Limerick, originally an Institute of Higher Education, where O'Malley is credited with taking the steps to ensure that it became a university. Access to third-level education was also extended, the old scholarship system being replaced by a system of means-tested grants that gave easier access to students whose parents could not afford the fees.

Shortly after O'Malley was appointed, he announced that from 1969 all education up to Intermediate Certificate level would be without cost, and free buses would bring students in rural areas to their nearest school. On 10 September 1966, in the Royal Marine Hotel in Dun Laoghaire, O'Malley addressed a dinner of the National Union of Journalists in which he publicly revealed his scheme:

'I propose therefore, from the coming school year, beginning in September of next year, to introduce a scheme whereby, up to the completion of the Intermediate Certificate course, the opportunity for free post-primary education will be available to all families.

This free education will be available in the comprehensive and vocational schools, and in the general run of secondary schools. I say the general run of secondary schools because there will still be schools, charging higher fees, who may not opt to take my scheme; and the parent who wants to send his child to one of these schools and pay the fees will of course be free to do so.

Going on from there, I intend also to make provision whereby no pupil will, for lack of means, be prevented from continuing his or her education up to the end of the Leaving Certificate course. Further, I propose that assistance towards the cost of books and accessories will be given, through the period of his or her course, to the student on whom it would be a hardship to meet all such costs.'

O'Malley's extension of free education to all certainly changed Ireland from a backward country where the majority were schooled only to the age of fourteen, to a country with universal secondary-school education, - this indirectly led to the Celtic Tiger boom of the 1990s-2000s. The 1967 Free Education Act ushered in a vast leap in education standards, and it was this that enabled the country to join the European Community in 1973 and the Celtic Tiger to happen a generation later. O'Malley certainly understood the educational requirements needed for any country to join the EU! And it was O'Malley who brought educational standards in Ireland into line in this respect.

And O'Malley was not the only man who was not afraid of McQuaid! Not the only man to understand how McQuaid and de Valera were holding Ireland back! Holding Ireland back with their isolationist policies, keeping Ireland free from outside influences! Keeping Ireland pure in the Catholic faith, - Catholicism Irish-style!

Keeping Ireland isolated and free from outside influences only resulted, as we saw earlier, in Irish people leaving the country in droves! The boats were full! Between 1945 and 1960, out of the total population of three and a half million people, over half a million Irish young people left, never to return. Left to find some sort of life and livelihood which was impossible to find in Ireland.

And who was that other man who was not afraid of McQuaid?

That other man was Thomas Kenneth Whitaker 1916 – 2017, an Irish economist, politician, diplomat and civil servant who served as Secretary of Ireland's Department of Finance from 1956 to 1969, as Governor of the Central Bank of Ireland from 1969 to 1976 and as a Senator from 1977 to 1982, after being nominated by the Taoiseach. He is considered one of the most influential civil servants in the history of the Irish State, with his economic policies greatly influencing the development of modern Ireland. In 1956, Whitaker was appointed Secretary of the Department of Finance, at the age of thirty-nine. His appointment took place at a time when Ireland's economy was in deep depression. Economic growth was non-existent, inflation apparently insoluble, unemployment rife, living standards low and emigration at a figure not far below the birth rate. Whitaker believed that free trade, with increased competition and the end of protectionism, would become inevitable and that jobs would have to be created by a shift from agriculture to industry and services. He formed a team of officials within the department which produced a detailed study of the economy, culminating in a plan recommending policies for improvement. The plan was accepted by the government and was transformed into a White Paper which became known as the First Programme for Economic Expansion, published in November 1958. The programme which became known as the *'Grey Book'* who many argue brought the stimulus of foreign investment into the Irish economy.

Whitaker's contribution included his championing of free trade over Ireland's previous disastrous policy of protectionism and his influencing of Taoiseach Jack Lynch to go down the free trade path, which resulted in the 1965 Anglo Irish Free Trade Bill. And it was Whitaker who persuaded the Irish Development Agency to seek out and target specific multinational companies, - pharmaceuticals, technology, medical equipment and financial companies, - and offer them very attractive terms to come to Ireland.

And so began the influx of companies investing in Ireland. First came

Microsoft in 1985; Intel in 1989; Motorola in 1989; Dell in 19990; HP in 1995; Oracle in 1996: Xerox in 1998 ; Cisco in 2007;

And the big banks followed! Citi Bank in 1996: Deutsche Bank in 1991; HSBC in 2000; MasterCard in 2009; PayPal in 2003.

And the communications networks! Google in 2003; Yahoo in 2003; eBay in 2004; Amazon in 2005; Facebook in 2008; Twitter in 2011; Linkedin in 2010; Electronic Arts in 2010; Zynga in 12010.

In 1973, Ireland had joined the European Economic Community, with a major financial boost for the Irish economy. If McQuaid had not just already died, this would surely have killed him!

The vision of both McQuaid and de Valera lay in tatters! The dream of de Valera that proved unattainable! The sands of time blowing over them, and burying them deeply, - just like the statue of Ozymandias in the desert! The winds of change! Nothing can stand against them! Not even the Catholic Church!

Although the denominational character of schools remained unaltered, a new balance of power in education had been achieved, in which the enhanced influence of the State in education was accepted with varying degrees of reluctance. During the 1990s and 2000s, there was a flurry of new policies in education by an increasingly interventionist and secular Irish State. For example, under the new primary school curriculum, introduced in 1999, there was a greater separation of secular and religious instruction than ever before. Under the 1998 Education Act, for the first time the State recognised a variety of nondenominational schools such as Gaelscoileanna, - Irish-language schools, - and multidenominational schools, which from 1984 came under the umbrella of Educate Together.

In September 2014, only ten religious, half of them women, served as principals of post primary schools compared to 104 in 1991. Religious orders withdrew almost entirely from the care of orphaned or neglected children during the 1990s and this was accelerated by revelations about abuse of many children in their care. At a parish level, the number of diocesan clergy declined sharply. In 2015 there were 1,966 active priests assigned to parish ministry, a fall of 1,010 since 2000 and almost half the 1961 total of 3,702. Alongside this crisis of vocations, census data revealed a steady decline in Catholic self-description amongst the laity. In 1981 the proportion of the population describing themselves as Catholic was 93 per cent, falling to 78.3 per cent in 2016, the lowest on record. The most noticeable finding in 2016 was that 9.8 per cent identified as *'No Religion'*.

The small agricultural, backward country of McQuaid and de Valera had become a country of a well-educated, skilled workforce, attracting foreign giant companies, supplying jobs, bringing a massive increase in living standards and wealth. And The Catholic Church was not in sight! The Catholic Church had no hand in it! In fact, indeed, the Catholic Church, under McQuaid and de Valera, had held Ireland back by decades!

And then came the final bomb-shell! The final nail in the coffin! The final kiss of death!

Revelations about paedophile scandals, cruel industrial schools and heartless Magdalene Mother-and-Baby homes for unmarried mothers, Magdalene laundries and asylums – in which Church and State seemed to collude, – prompted a wave of hostility against what remained of the dominance of Catholic Church power.

And a whole new generation was emerging! A new generation that did not share the same religious beliefs of their ancestors. Surveys showed that amongst those who had left for America, the majority did not even attend regular mass.

By the centenary of 1916, same-sex marriage and abortion rights were on the national agenda. Ireland was an altered state and outright hostility to

Catholicism was often evident. By 2021, a government video about St. Patrick's Day erased all mention of St. Patrick himself, lest it *'contaminate'* the brand of a new Ireland.

And yes, even the forename of *'Mary'*, once so common that half the class at any convent school bore it, is now a highly unusual name among younger generations.

The Catholic Church has found itself in a battle it cannot win, - trying to hold up the walls of Catholicism.

But those walls came tumbling down! The wonder is that they had stood intact for so long!

Chapter 7

And the walls came tumbling down

We have just seen how various and specific social and economic developments led to a rapid decline in the power of the Catholic Church in Ireland. If we were to prioritise and try and decide which one had the greatest impact, then I would argue that it was the coming of television and the internet. The economic boom, with its materialism and commercialisation, and the cleric sex scandals just put the last nails in the Catholic Church coffin!

Television and the internet that opened Ireland up to world influences! Information that had up to now been kept from us now suddenly was available to all at the press of a button! And it was not good news for the Catholic Church!

And then came the scandals, tumbling out in free fall! Scandals on a massive scale, obvious hypocrisy on a massive scale, lies, denials, deceit and cover-ups on a massive scale - these all played their part in bringing about the loss of moral authority of the Catholic Church and the loss of respect of the laity in Ireland for their priests and religious. The total, complete and unquestioning trust, the blind obedience that Irish people had placed in their Church, in their priests and religious, was now broken. And that is the thing about such complete and unquestioning trust, - once it is broken, it cannot be retrieved! Gone! Gone for good!

But that loss of trust had begun even before the scandals about cleric child abuse broke! The coming of the internet was not good news for the Catholic Church! Revealing as it did that what we had always been taught was not the truth! The discovery of the Nag Hammadi Scripts in 1945 in the desert in Egypt, - hidden to escape the purges ordered by the Christian Church to get rid of all other gospels which did not fit their agenda, - and the Dead Sea Scrolls, all started off a mass awakening! A mass realisation that the four canonical gospels were not written by the followers of Jesus, Matthew being the scribe, copying down what Jesus was saying; that the gospels were not written at the reputed time of Jesus, but by the Romans as a means of propaganda against the Jews in their conquered Roman territories; that Christianity was begun by the Romans in the fourth century, and not with Jesus; that the gospels were full of contradictions and anomalies; that Jesus had brothers and sisters; that Peter, who became the first pope, was married, - Jesus went to cure Peter's mother-in law; that Mary Magdalene was not the prostitute, the *'fallen woman',* but the sexual partner of Yeshua, - his name was Yeshua, - teaching alongside him in his ministry as part of the secretive Essene Community in Jewish Palestine 2,000 years ago.

And then we discovered that the whole *'story'* of Christianity, the birth of Jesus, born of a virgin on December 25th, dying on the cross to save humanity, is simply a rehash of the ancient religion of Judaism, which in turn is simply a rehash of the ancient Egyptian beliefs and dogmas! Yes, Jesus was just the last *'God'* in a long line of ancient Greek and Roman *'gods'* to be born of a virgin on 25th December, at the winter solstice and then to die for humanity! Jesus was not unique! This ancient *'story',* and that is what it is, a *'story',* is all written in the stars, in astromythology, permeating unchecked down through the centuries to us today, in this, the 21st century! That's why we were never encouraged to read the gospels for ourselves! That's why we were never allowed to get our fortune told, or read the *'stars'* in the newspapers, - that was a mortal sin! We might find out something! That's why everything we *'needed to know'* was thundered out to us from the pulpit! And all of this I have documented and explained fully in three specific previous books**, 'The Almost Immaculate Deception! The Greatest Scam in History?'; 'And That's The Gospel Truth!'; and 'The Truth Will Set You Free: Christianity? - Where Did It all Begin?'** - all available on Amazon Books.

And discovering that we had been lied to all along, - that was when the trust was broken! So even if the clerical sex abuse scandals had never surfaced, the power of the Catholic Church in Ireland was on the fast decline anyway! The pope's visit in 1979 showed something was wrong! As already mentioned in the previous chapter, survey findings have indicated that the higher the level of educational attainment, the lower the level of orthodox religious belief and acceptance of Church teaching. And the internet certainly was educating us! So in this sense the papal visit in 1979, when an estimated 2.7 million people greeted John Paul II, was less a celebration of Catholic Ireland than an unsuccessful attempt to slow down the inroads made by materialism and secularism, - and by education!

And then when we thought we were immune to any more shocks, out poured the information about the Magdalene institutions!

And we cannot overlook the contribution of the media in exposing religious institutions which, as we have seen earlier, were once above public scrutiny! Investigative journalism has played a major role in uncovering clerical sexual and religious institutional scandals and televised documentaries such as BBC2 in 2002, 'Suing the Pope' and RTE in 2002, 'Cardinal Secrets' prompted the establishment of inquiries. Inquiries which led to harrowing reports such as the Ferns report in 2005, the Ryan report and the Murphy report, both in 2009, and the Cloyne report in 2011, among others. The Cloyne report prompted an unprecedented condemnation of the Vatican by Taoiseach Enda Kenny in the Dáil, and In November 2011 the Irish government decided to close its Vatican embassy, reputedly on economic grounds; it was subsequently reopened in 2014.

And then - yet another earth-shattering shock! Another shocking blow to an already stunned Irish nation! The shocking realisation that sexual abuse and rape by priests and bishops was rife in Ireland! And had been going on for quite some time! And all covered up by the Church hierarchy! And the Irish government knew all about it! All shrouded in secrecy! To quote Owen Felix O'Neill, website *tuambabies.org,* who himself spent the first eighteen years of his life in state industrial schools:

'Secrecy is an Irish disease, secrecy is also a Catholic Church sacred ritual, the Catholic Church thrives on secrecy......the Secrecy was suppressed for many decades and was orchestrated and perpetuated by both the Irish Catholic Church, its Clerics, further concealed and encouraged with the active help of most members of the Irish Government at the time.' (Owen Felix O'Neill, *tuambabies.org* in an article on 26th September 2021, under the title *'What's in a name - Artane Boys Band'*)

The clerical sex abuse scandals and the Church's inadequate response have all been intensely corrosive! Truly, there is no way back!

How could any institution possibly survive against all of that? And the answer? It cannot! And despite all the good work done by various members of the Catholic Church! Because they were not all rotten apples in the proverbial barrel!

And it was not just in Ireland!

On Tuesday 16th August 2016, RTE broadcast a programme called *'Scandal at the Vatican: The Legionaries of Christ'.* This was an investigation into the life of Marciel Maciel, a Mexican priest who founded the *'Legionaries of Christ'* in 1941, and remained as its director until 2006, when he was finally removed from his position by the Vatican. Maciel died in 2008.

Copious documentation was presented to the Vatican in the 1940s and 50s, complaining about dubious morals, drug use, financial recklessness and sexual abuse of Maciel's young seminarians. Yet it took the Holy See more than a half-century to sanction Maciel, and even more for it to acknowledge he was a religious fraud and con artist who molested his seminarians, fathered three children and built a secretive, cult-like religious order to hide his double life. The death of Pope Pius in 1958 interrupted investigations into Maciel's activities, - Pope Pius about to sanction Maciel, including removing him from priestly office altogether.

In 2012, some of Maciel's Mexican victims put online 200-plus documents spanning the 1940s-2002 that they had obtained from someone with access to the Congregation for Religious archive. These documents, also in the book *'La Voluntad De No Saber'* - meaning *'The Will to Not Know'*, detailed the evidence the Vatican had of Maciel's depravities, but also how decades of bishops, cardinals and popes turned a blind eye and believed instead the glowing reports of Maciel that also arrived in Rome.

Former members of Maciel's *'Legionaries of Christ'* have described how the society was run like a secretive cult. Maciel himself led a double life as a paedophile, womaniser and drug abuser, establishing into the society the notorious vow never to criticise Maciel himself, creating a *'code of silence'* culture in the Legion. That culture of silence again!

During his directorship, Maciel drew thousands of young men into the priesthood and sizeable financial donations to the Catholic Church. The Legionaries of Christ Society was noted for its dynamic growth and fund-raising prowess, and it had many wealthy conservative benefactors who saw it as a bulwark against liberation in the Church. Maciel himself was acknowledged by the Vatican as *'The greatest fundraiser of the modern Roman Catholic Church',* and praised lavishly for his prolific recruitment of new seminarians.

When complaints reached the Vatican, of course they were covered up, as was the channeling of large sums of money to favoured Vatican officials, as reported in NCR in 2009.

Maciel's behaviour, including the sex scandals and bestial acts with young seminarians, although described by those who reported them to the Vatican as *'reprehensible and objectively immoral behaviour'*, was not investigated by the Vatican, Cardinal Ratzinger himself covering up for him, saying that Maciel had done so much good for the Church, and to bring this out now, with the

Pope, John Paul II in failing health, would be very upsetting. The case was closed.

And Maciel's explanation for his bestial acts of abuse? He claimed that he had permission from Pope Pius XII to engage in sexual activity with the young seminarians in order to relieve the pain of his stomach ulcer! And this was the same man who accompanied Pope John Paul II to Mexico, not just on one occasion, but three times, in 1979, 1990 and 1993!

Despite knowing about the accusations against him, what did the Church hierarchy in Rome do about it? They did what they always do! They closed clerical ranks against the scandal! Pope John Paul II himself publicly acknowledged Maciel as '*an efficacious guide to youth*', and as late as 2004, congratulated him for his '*intense, generous, and fruitful priestly ministry*'.

The wonder is that he did not recommend him as the next pope!

But in late 2004, Ratzinger finally ordered an investigation into Maciel. The international scandal that stained Ratzinger's term as Pope Benedict stems from an archaic justice system that gives cardinals and bishops de facto immunity from persecution.

And who was friendly with Maciel? - None other than Archbishop John Charles McQuaid! Archbishop John Charles McQuaid, during whose term of ecclesiastical office in Ireland the Magdalene institutions and the Industrial Schools flourished, prospered and thrived, - with all the sexual abuse against children! The Magdalene Mother-and-Baby homes, the Magdalene Laundries and the Magdalene Asylums. And I have dealt with these Magdalene Institutions fully in my previous book, '**WHAT'S IN A NAME? THE MAGDALENE INSTITUTIONS IN 20th CENTURY IRELAND. - Refuge, reform or punishment?**'

From 1922 to 1996 in Ireland alone, over 10,000 young women were forced into these institutions, condemned by the Church as '*fallen women*' for their '*shameful pregnancies*', their '*errors of the flesh*'. Deprived of their own identities and any sort of freedom, their new-born babies removed and sold to wealthy families chosen by the nuns, these young women were treated as criminals, forced into hard labour in sweated laundries, supervised and guarded by merciless, sadistic nuns whose vindictiveness knew no bounds. Women condemned to a life of cruelty and brutality simply at the word of a priest! Women subjected to societal shame and degradation! And so many of them victims of rape, incest, sexual abuse and rape by priests and bishops!

The first wave of clerical sexual scandal in Ireland involved paternity cases, - that of Eamon Casey, Bishop of Galway, in 1992, and shortly afterwards, that of Fr. Michael Cleary, - the same two very high-profile, jovial, singing clerics who had been chosen to entertain the crowds gathered in Galway for the visit of Pope John Paul in 1979.

The discovery that Eamon Casey, who served as Bishop of Kerry 1969-1976, and then as Bishop of Galway and Kilmacduagh from 1976 to 1992, had secretly fathered a child with an American woman, Annie Murphy, in the 1970s and used Church funds to support her, stunned the Irish nation. His resignation as bishop and his removal in 1992 was most certainly a pivotal moment in the Irish nation's relationship with the Catholic Church.

Casey's constant refusal to acknowledge his son, his determination that the child should be given up for adoption in order to avoid any scandal for himself or the Catholic Church, and his embezzlement of Church funds for his son's maintenance was what was most shocking. At a conference for *'Cherish'*, - an Irish Catholic charity established to support unmarried mothers, Casey had said: *'It is difficult to understand how the total rejection of their child . . . could be reconciled with Christian love and forgiveness'*. Yet of his own son, he told Annie Murphy, *'He is not my son. He's entirely yours now'*.

The hypocrisy of it all! That's what was shocking! But despite that, there were those who supported him. After all, as a human being, as a man, what he had done in fathering a child was natural. In the eyes of many, he had just failed to adhere to his vow of chastity, - and anyway, the vow of clerical celibacy was a

Catholic-Church-only imposed vow!

In the early 1990s Annie Murphy contacted the Irish Times to tell the truth about Casey's hypocrisy and deception. Having been exposed, Casey reluctantly admitted that he had '*sinned*' and wronged the boy, his mother and '*God, his church and the clergy and people of the dioceses of Galway and Kerry*', and his embezzlement of church funds. He was forced to resign as bishop, and fled the country under a cloud of scandal. Murphy's book '*Forbidden Fruit*', published in 1993 revealed the truth about their relationship and the son she bore by Casey, exposing the institutional level of hypocrisy, moral corruption and misogyny within the Irish Catholic Church. Because it was not just Casey himself on trial here in the minds of the Irish people, but the Catholic Church itself.

Casey, condemned by many as a '*cad*', was ordered by the Vatican to leave Ireland, and became a missionary alongside members of the Missionary Society of St. James in a rural parish in Ecuador, whose language, Spanish, he did not speak. During this time, he travelled long distances to reach the widely scattered members of his parish, but did not travel to meet his own son. After his missionary position was completed, he took a position in the parish of St. Pauls, Haywards Heath, in south-east England.

In 2005, Casey was investigated in conjunction with a sexual abuse scandal in Galway, Kilmacduagh and Kilfenora diocese, and cleared of any wrongdoing. He returned to Ireland in 2006 with his reputation in tatters, and was not permitted to say mass in public.

A number of women made allegations to the state and to the Church against Casey, during his life, that they had been sexually abused by him. Two of these women received compensation following a High Court trial. One of the women, his niece Patricia Donovan, alleged in 2005, and again in 2019, that she was raped by Casey when she was five years old and assaulted sexually by him for more than a decade.

In August 2011, in poor health, Casey was admitted to a nursing home in County Clare. He died on 13 March 2017, aged 89.

So that was the end of Casey! Or so we all thought! For many years his fathering of a son with Annie Murphy was the most controversial thing known about him.

But it was not the end of Casey! It was what emerged after his death that shocked the Irish nation even more than the scandal during his lifetime! In 2019, it emerged that he had faced at least three accusations of sexual abuse before his death, with two High Court cases being settled. The Kerry diocese confirmed that it had received allegations against him, that Gardaí and health authorities had been informed and that the person concerned was offered support by the diocese. These independent accusations relate to alleged events in every Irish diocese where Casey worked.

One of the women, his niece Patricia Donovan, alleged in 2019 that she was repeatedly raped by Casey when she was five years old and assaulted sexually by him for more than a decade. Writing in The Irish Times, historian Diarmaid Ferriter described Casey as *'a sexist hypocrite'*, the Herald reported that he *'liked fast cars... and was banned for drink driving'*, and numerous outlets reported on his fraudulent use of Church funds amounting to hundreds of thousands of pounds.

Just recently, on Monday 22nd July 2024, RTE aired a documentary *'Bishop Casey's Buried Secrets'*, examining the Catholic Church's handling of allegations against Bishop Casey. The investigation also confirmed that Bishop Casey was formally removed from public ministry in 2007 by the Vatican, following *'allegations'* which, RTÉ established, included his niece's complaint of child sexual abuse. That restriction continued for the last ten years of his but life but was never publicly disclosed in Casey's lifetime.

Despite his resignation as Bishop of Galway in 1992, he remained a bishop until his death in 2017 and claimed his removal from ministry was *'unjust'*. In

2019, when the Irish Daily Mail asked the Galway Diocese how many allegations of child sexual abuse had been made against Casey, they were told there was one. However, the documentary which was made in collaboration with the newspaper revealed that in 2019 there were *'five people who had complained of childhood sexual abuse against Bishop Casey'.*

'Bishop Casey's Buried Secrets' included an interview with one of the former Bishop's accusers, his niece Patricia Donovan, who claimed that Casey first raped her at the age of five and that the sexual abuse continued for years.

Speaking for the first time on camera, Ms O'Donovan said: *'Some of the things he did to me, and where he did them... the horror of being raped by him when I was five, the violence. And it just carried on in that vein... He had no fear of being caught........He thought he could do what he liked, when he liked, how he liked......He was almost, like, incensed that I would dare fight against him, that I would dare try and hurt him, I would dare try and stop him...... It didn't make any difference...'*

However, as the RTE programme pointed out, the Vatican has declined to say what investigative process was followed or whether the sanctions it imposed on Bishop Casey were punitive or precautionary.

'Bishop Casey's Buried Secrets' also revealed how the Limerick Diocese paid over €100,000 in settlement to one of Bishop Casey's accusers after Casey's death.

And the programme raised serious questions not just about Casey, but about the Vatican and the Catholic Church. The former CEO of the National Board for Safeguarding Children in the Irish Catholic Church described the former Bishop of Galway Eamonn Casey as 'a *sexual predator',* and, having direct knowledge of Ms Donovan's complaint against Casey, he found her account of what she experienced *'entirely credible'.* And journalist and author Conor Pope shared a personal experience with the former bishop, *'I grew up in Galway and met Eamonn Casey often. He sat in on school retreats, lecturing us on morality.....I was an intern in the Connacht Tribune when the story broke. Despite the scandal and endless hypocrisy, I always thought he wasn't the worst of them. I don't think that now.'*

The documentary also included friends, colleagues and supporters, who still find it hard to believe the allegations made against Casey.

And the funeral he was given? Why was he allowed that particular one? Why were the funeral arrangements specified by the Vatican for sex-abusing bishops not put in place? Why was he allowed to be buried in the crypt of Galway Cathedral? How had he been able to officiate at the burial service and conduct the recent funeral of his niece's mother? The mother of the niece he had raped? And how was he able to perform a baptismal service shortly afterwards?

And now, the Galway diocese has just issued a statement saying that after the RTE programme was aired, so many people questioned why Casey is buried in the crypt of Galway Cathedral, that proceedings and discussions have now begun about the matter of his burial.

The programme was not just an indictment of Eamon Casey, but an indictment of the whole of the Catholic Church! The secrecy, the cover-ups, the closing of ranks, the scandals! The whole operations of the Vatican looked like a cult! Especially when the camera showed a shot from the back of the huge room where the bishops were assembled in a meeting of the Congress of Bishops. All those scarlet skull caps! And black ensembles! It certainly got across the power of the Catholic Church and the extent of its outage and outreach! And yes, one could have been forgiven for thinking, - very '*cult-like*'!

Shortly after Eamon Casey was exposed, it emerged in 1995 that his friend and colleague, Fr. Michael Cleary had fathered two children. Cleary, the high-profile media figure well-known for his defence of traditional Catholic values. And more than a year after his death, the revelation that he had been leading a double life, - the life of a high-profile celibate priest, and a hidden private life with his housekeeper, Phyllis Hamilton, with whom he had fathered two children, one of whom was placed for adoption.

But the tsunami had started from the late '80s and early '90s onwards. And this was not just about priests and bishops fathering children! This was about horrifying sexual abuse of young children by priests and higher clergy. And priests being found in gay clubs in Dublin. The owner of the *'Incognito Sauna Club'* in Bowe Lane, off Dublin's Aungier Street, confirmed that priests made up a significant number of the club's membership.

And so it went on and on! The Irish nation growing accustomed to the daily newspapers reporting sex charges against Catholic clergy. Sexual abuse, indecent assault, rape, buggery, pornographic photographs of young children, - all relentless and horrifying!

Probably the most notorious of all was the Brendan Smyth scandal which hit the headlines in 1991. Brendan Smyth, the incorrigible Norbertine Order paedophile priest, for whom religious authorities had been covering up for a number of years! Everywhere he went, everywhere he served, he left a devastating trail of destruction behind him. At a time when priests were held in the highest esteem and regarded with the highest reverence in Ireland, above and beyond suspicion, Smyth continued to rape young children even when their parents were also present there in the house, and never suspecting a thing. And it was John Charles McQuaid who ordained Smyth in July 1951, despite complaints about him having abused a child when he was a student in Rome in the 1940s, and despite advice from the abbot general of the Norbertines in Rome that Smyth should not actually be ordained. For over forty years after his ordination, Smyth, under the guise and security of the priesthood, continued to rape and sexually abuse young children, many of whom later took their own lives.

Despite sheltering in his monastery at Holy Trinity Abbey in Ballyjamesduff, County Cavan, Smyth was eventually charged in Belfast, convicted and imprisoned. The total number of his helpless victims will probably never be known but it ran into hundreds, spread over six different jurisdictions, - Ireland, including Northern Ireland, Italy, Scotland, Wales and the USA, where he operated in Rhode Island, North Dakota and Boston. And always arrogantly secure in the knowledge that his Irish superiors would not reveal his activities!

Following his death in prison, he was buried at dark of night, encased in concrete, with the title of *'Father'* excluded from the gravestone, in the Norbertine graveyard near Ballyjamesduff. And buried with him was the tattered remains of the reputation of the once so dominant Catholic Church in Ireland. A Catholic Church that had deliberately chosen to protect and cover up for a malicious, ferocious, insatiable, predatory paedophile. And two cardinals would be held to account! Cardinal Cahal Daly and Cardinal Sean Brady who actively covered up for him. Cahal Daly who knew about the abuses and did nothing about it, except write letters to one of Smyth's victims in 1990 and 1992, offering sympathy, admitting he knew about Smyth's activities, but he could do nothing about it. Probably because it was up to the head of the Norbertines to discipline Smyth, and not the bishop of the diocese.

Sean Brady, at the time, a young teacher in St. Partrick' College Cavan, and who was later to succeed Cahal Daly as Cardinal, was appointed to investigate the charges made against Smyth in 1975. One boy, Brendan Boland described how Brady and two others who questioned him were hostile, asking him if he enjoyed masturbation, inferring that if he did, then he must therefore have enjoyed being abused by Smyth. Brendan's father was excluded from the interview, which was entirely concerned with trapping Brendan into some sort of admission that he was the guilty party and not Smyth! None of the questions asked ever suggested any sort of concern for his emotional or mental welfare.

Brady always claimed that he was nothing more than a note-taker, but it later transpired that he was in fact the senior canon lawyer in the group. Brady swore Boland to secrecy. For eighteen years after Brady had been informed of Smyth's activities, nothing was done about him. It was the Northern Ireland police force who eventually stepped in.

Sworn to secrecy! The culture of secrecy, under the euphemism *confidentiality* that was so all-powerful at that time, concerned first and foremost with protecting and keeping intact the reputation of the Catholic Church! Brady's loyalty to that same Catholic Church, and his unquestioning obedience to Church hierarchy was unshakable. So there would be no report by Brady to police authorities, no follow-up by Brady into how the Church was intending to discipline Brady, - if indeed at all! Brady has always insisted that there was no legal obligation on him to do anything more than he did. In other words, he stuck to the rule book! He followed the Church procedure! And in doing so, he did nothing wrong!

Both Daly and Brady were forced into retirement under the dark cloud of having covered up serious sexual clerical abuse. And Bishop John Magee, who had been so prominent in the pope's visit to Ireland in 1979 was also to retire in disgrace, after the Cloyne Report in 2011 declared him guilty of covering up and not passing on allegations of child abuses to the authorities.

And it was not just senior clergy who were destroyed by the Brendan Smyth case. We saw earlier how the Catholic Church under Cardinal Paul Cullen was able to take down Charles Stuart Parnell and how Archbishop John Charles McQuaid was able to take down Noel Browne. So, now too, the Brendan Smyth case took down the Irish Government, under Taoiseach Albert Reynolds. How? - Reynolds appointed Attorney General Harry Whelehan to the position of President of the High Court. The very same conservative Catholic Harry Whelehan who was believed to have tried to cover up for the Church by delaying the request for the extradition of Smyth. Reynolds refused to back down, and the government collapsed in the face of the anger of its coalition partners, the Labour Party.

And indeed, it could be said that Brendan Smyth, one man on his own, did more than any other man to destroy the Catholic Church.

In 1995 another notorious Irish paedophile priest was exposed, - Father Sean Fortune! Father Sean Fortune who took his own life in 1999, at the start of his trial, rather than face the condemnation and punishment that was finally coming to him!

Father Sean Fortune who served in County Wexford! And this time it was Brendan Comiskey, Bishop of Ferns, who ended up in the direct firing line! Comiskey who eventually ended up in America for treatment for his serious alcohol addiction. Fortune's story is told by Alison O'Connor in her book *'A Message From Heaven - The Life and Crimes of Father Sean Fortune'*. The title coming from the fact that he left behind him a poem which he had titled *'A Message from Heaven to my Family'*.

Fortune was not only guilty of sexual abuse and rape of children, - that was indeed his worst and most prolific crime. But he was also known to be a cheat, a swindler of Church finances, a manipulator, a liar and a bully, amassing great sums of money through various farcical means. Some of his activities would indeed have put Chaucer's notorious Canterbury Tales Church characters, - the Pardoner and Summoner, - into the shadow! He ran his own money-making empire, undisturbed, from Fethard-on Sea in County Wexford, where he controlled everything, groomed and molested young boys, and manipulated and bullied parishioners into doing what he wanted, - mostly swindling them into parting with huge sums of money for this, that or the other of his dubious schemes. Parishioners made specific, repeated and urgent complaints to various clerics about Fortune and to Bishop Comiskey, but no action was taken. No surprise there!

Fortune was ordained in May 1979. His first year as a priest was spent in Belfast, based at Holy Rosary Church, and while there, he would often visit Nazareth House orphanage in the south of the city, - the same orphanage frequented by Brendan Smyth, where Smyth abused children when he was left alone with them in the visitors' room. Fortune's next parish was Dundalk, where he held *'Youth Encounter'* retreats, and then in 1981 he was appointed curate to Poulfour in Fethard-on-Sea in South Wexford, where he continued to molest young boys, - and Bishop Herlihy knew about it! Fortune established his authority right from the start, tolerating no opposition or challenging, and setting up numerous groups and trips, mostly for young people. He had no shortage of money, - with an apartment in Dublin and sporting fast, flashy big cars. He constantly invited young boys to his house, where they slept in his bed with him, making them swear that they would not tell anyone what happened. He lured them in with money and treats, promising them anything they wanted, and threatened them all to remain quiet.

And so it went on! In 1985 Bishop Comiskey confirming that he had directed Fortune to attend a psychologist. Then he was moved to Ballymurn, a small village between Gorey and Wexford. And there he continued his pattern of control, manipulation and abuse. He established courses in media studies, with modules, exams and certificates, all copied from various sources, drawing people in for large fees, harassing them and bullying them, and pretending his media studies modules were approved by various institutions, including RTE.

After numerous complaints, Fortune was removed from Ballymurn by Bishop Comiskey in March 1995. He disappeared to Dublin, where he continued to make money through his fake courses. But time ran out for him! And in March, 1999, after an investigation had been opened, he appeared in Wexford District Court. Accused of numerous sexual abuses, including buggery, with witnesses coming forward from as far back as 1979, Fortune must have realised that his game was up. His suicide on 11th March 1999, deprived his victims of ever looking him straight in the eye and being able to say *'you did this to me'*.

His funeral in Gorey was attended by around 140 people, in St. Patrick's Church. Alison O'Connor, in her book *'A Message From Heaven - The Life and Crimes of Father Sean Fortune'* describes how the priests sat together on one side of the church, *'their discomfort was evident, being made worse by the large gathering of media outside the door. Their clerical garb made them obvious targets for photographers........there was no pride that day in wearing priests' collars.'* ('A Message From Heaven', Alison O'Connor, page 230)

So, the end of Sean Fortune! But there is never an end to cases like this! **Cause** and **Effect** and all that! The ripples reverberate and permeate downwards and outwards! And again, as in all the other cases of clerical sexual abuse, it is the Catholic Church that is under severe scrutiny! And rightly so! Abusers like Smyth and Fortune should have been locked away. What excuse does the Catholic Church have for not making this happen? Why were men like Smyth and Fortune continuously left to prey freely on vulnerable children, continuously placed in positions of authority where they had free and uninhibited access to children? And despite Church hierarchy knowing about them! And despite the warnings the hierarchy got about these men before they were ever ordained!

Places where there is access to children! One obviously thinks first of schools! And yes, in the last years of the 1990s and the opening years of the new millennium, scandals continued to pour out from schools all around the country!

Blackrock College in South County Dublin! That most prestigious of boarding schools for boys! Made famous as a place of special importance in all Catholic Church celebrations by John Charles McQuaid!

In 2022, new allegations of child sexual abuse by priests at Blackrock College emerged, after a radio documentary on RTE 1, Monday 7th November 2022, that told in detail of two brothers who were sexually abused by priests at the school in the 1970s and early 1980s, neither of them aware that the same was happening to both of them.

From the ages of 12 to 17, they were both repeatedly sexually abused both in and on the grounds of Blackrock College, by members of the community of the Holy Ghost order, now known as Spiritans. The abuse took place in the college library, the swimming pool and other buildings.

Several court cases ensued as they fought for justice. Now grown men, they told their story for the first time in that special RTÉ 1 Documentary, broadcast at 6.00 pm on Monday 7th November, breaking the national radio schedule for the final hour of 'Drivetime'. The two men named publicly in the documentary were the first people to openly speak about abuse at Blackrock College.

The older brother began his secondary education at Blackrock College in September 1973. During his first year, one of the teachers, a Holy Ghost father, took a special interest in him and gradually began to sexually abuse him, during private swimming lessons at the pool on the college campus. Another priest from Blackrock College also began to abuse the boy. Throughout his abuse, the boy never told anyone.

The second brother was 12, when he first began to be invited by the same priest to swimming sessions on the grounds of Blackrock College and over the next number of years he too was repeatedly sexually abused.

For many years neither brother spoke of their abuse, until early 2002 when clerical child sex abuse filled the news headlines. This led the brothers to reveal their abuse, first to their parents, and then to one another. They made statements to An Garda Síochána which led to multiple charges being brought against their abuser.

By then the Holy Ghost priest was 82 years old and still living on the grounds of Blackrock College. He denied the charges made against him and launched a legal case, seeking to halt criminal proceedings. In 2007, the courts decided that the criminal case against the brothers' abuser should be halted. The abuser died in 2010, having never had to face trial.

Indeed, the number of children who were sexually abused on the grounds of Blackrock College is unknown. Holy Ghost records now indicate that 233 people have made allegations of abuse against 77 Irish Holy Ghost fathers in ministries throughout Ireland and overseas. In relation to Blackrock College, 57 people have alleged they were abused on the Blackrock campus.

The Holy Ghost community have made multiple monetary contributions to people who have alleged abuse at the hands of Spiritan community members – and since 2004 the total amount paid by them, in settlement of claims of abuse, and towards support services, amounts to over €5 million.

In 2012, the Holy Ghost fathers issued a general apology having been heavily criticised in an audit reviewing Child Protection practices. This audit also detailed how serial abusers within the Spiritans went undetected and unchecked, giving them unmonitored access to children during the 1960s, '70s and '80s.

The RTE documentary made known that at least 233 men had made allegations of abuse against 77 Irish priests from the Holy Ghost Fathers, some of whom were serial abusers left with unchecked access to children in the 1960s, 1970s and 1980s.

One of the named abusing priests, originally from Limerick, took up teaching roles at St. Michael's College in Dublin in 1962 before moving to Blackrock College in 1967. School records show he was still listed as a member of the school community until at least 1996/97. He faced multiple charges of child sexual abuse during the 2000s. A number of past pupils say they were abused by him in the school's swimming pool and in the priest's quarters. The Director of Public Prosecutions charged him with 37 offences arising out of sexual abuse but in 2007 the Supreme Court dismissed it on the basis that the priest was then 87. He died in 2010.

Another of the reputed abusing priests was appointed to Blackrock College in 1957 and became a teacher in Willow Park School. He played a key role in coaching junior rugby teams. When he retired from teaching, he stayed on as a member of the college community until at least the late 1990s. One past-pupil who was abused by him at 12 years of age, said he had easy access to boarders and describes him as *'rapacious'*. Another says he went to the headmaster of Blackrock College at the time and ended up in a meeting with the headmaster, the priest and his parents in which the accused denied any abuse. He died in 2004. And this particular victim ended up later in life as a heroin addict.

And a third accused abusing priest, from Ballyhaunis, Co Mayo, was a former student of Blackrock College. He was appointed as a teacher at Willow Park in the primary section of the school in 1960 and worked in various roles until 1977. One past pupil recalls being woken up one night and seriously sexually assaulted by Flood. *'I was a pious, innocent 11-year-old asleep in my bed, boarding at Willow Park. I had no idea what was going on'*. This priest was later appointed principal of St Michael's in 1977 before returning to Blackrock College in 1983 as dean of the boarding school. He spent a number of years as a curate in Dalkey parish in the 1990s. He died in 2013.

And a Brother, from Clogher, County Tyrone, joined Blackrock College initially as a gardener in 1950 before securing a teaching role in Willow Park in 1955-1995. He taught religion and had responsibility for Holy Communion classes. One past pupil, who served as an altar boy, describes being groomed and later abused. 'I resisted as best I could,' he recalls. 'And that was when the anger came into it. The violence. The first time he raped me the pain was unbelievable – he did it in rage'. The Brother left the school community around 2000, and died in 2002.

So abuse after abuse after abuse! A tsunami pouring out from all places, anywhere and anywhere that gave access to children.

But! At the same time, and however difficult it may indeed be, we must also accept the reality that despite the rapid decline in the power of the Catholic Church in Ireland, we cannot deny the huge amount of work done for the less well-off in society by many priests and religious. Because they were not all abusing and molesting! They were not all rotten apples!

In 1969, for example, Brother Kevin Crowley founded the Capuchin Day Center in Dublin to provide food and clothing, along with personal care facilities for those in need. In 1978, Brother Donal O'Mahony, another Capuchin, founded *'Threshold',* to address housing inequality, deprivation, and insufficient legislative protection for tenants. In 1983 Peter McVerry, a Jesuit, founded the *'Peter McVerry Trust'* to tackle homelessness, drugs, and social disadvantage. He is arguably the best known and most outspoken advocate of greater equality and social inclusion. In 1985 Sister Stanislaus Kennedy of the Sisters of Charity was a co-founder of *'Focus Ireland',* a housing charity. She later established the Immigrant Council of Ireland.

And from the 1970s indeed, the Church hierarchy was vocal about the interlinked problems of poverty, long-term unemployment, and emigration, as well as the inadequacy of Ireland's social infrastructure. The bishops of the west of Ireland were proactive in commissioning a major jobs and regional development study to stem unemployment and emigration; this was published in 1994 as *'Crusade for Survival'.* It led to a public campaign and the establishment, three years later, of the Western Development Commission as a government agency. Aside from economic issues, members of the hierarchy addressed a broad range of social problems, including, among others, drug abuse and alcoholism, the commercialisation of Sunday, responsible advertising, suicide, and discrimination against the Travelling community.

And then there are the voluntary organisations led by religious, or under religious patronage, such as the Society of St Vincent de Paul, all tackling socio-economic issues in our society. Society of St. Vincent de Paul, which has been working quietly to ameliorate the consequences of poverty since the 1840s, with no song and dance! And in modern times tackling wide-spread social deprivation, unemployment, poverty, limited social services, homelessness, drugs and alcoholism. And Trócaire, the bishops' overseas development agency established in 1973, paralleled these efforts through aid to the developing world.

And McQuaid! We must acknowledge that McQuaid too, did a lot of good!

Social reforms, establishment of schools and hospitals, founding of all sorts of clubs and societies to make people feel involved and useful.

And the religious orders who taught us all! The religious orders who devoted their lives to teaching and caring for the sick and dying!

And Eamon Casey! All the good that he too did for society! Working alongside and aiding Irish emigrants in Britain! Campaigning while a young priest in England in housing the homeless and acting as director of the Catholic Housing Aid Society in Westminster which did not only assist Catholics. Helping to found *'Shelter'* in 1966, the charity for the homeless. Helping to set up *'Trocaire',* which provided aid to developing countries. Championing the rights of the Irish Travelling community. Working with 'Cherish', a support group for unmarried mothers. In addition, supporting Dunnes Stores' staff who were locked out from 1982 to 1986 for refusing to sell goods from apartheid South Africa. He became a vocal opponent of United States foreign policy in Central America, and, as a result, opposed the 1984 visit of United States President Ronald Reagan to Ireland, refusing to meet him when he came to Galway.

While in Galway, Casey was seen as a progressive, a significant change in a diocese that had been led for nearly forty years by the very conservative Michael Browne, Bishop from 1937 to 1976.

And Fr. Michael Cleary! The best-known priest in Ireland! And for all the right reasons! An energetic worker in the vast Dublin suburb of Crumlin, and later in Griffith Avenue. He who brought cheer and joy into so many people's lives with his singing and guitar playing, running bingo events and cabaret shows in parish halls and community centres. Supporting unmarried mothers. Helping the Irish emigrant community in London when he was a curate there. Co-founder of the *'All Priests' Show',* giving charity performance around the country. Working with those who had been transplanted to Ballyfermot from the inner-city slums.

But all of this was not enough to hold up the crumbling edifice!

And the Walls Came Tumbling Down!

It was the hypocrisy that offended people the most! The double lives that were being led! The very ones who were preaching to us from the pulpit were breaking their own rules! And had been doing so for a long time!

And the edifice crumbled from the top down! That same patriarchal, authoritarian, Catholic Church that enjoyed a lengthy heyday in Ireland from the 1920s to the 1960s or even 1980s, was now in free fall!

William Butler Yeats wrote: *'Too long a sacrifice can make a stone of the heart.'*

Meaning that denying natural basic human instincts, - such as imposed celibacy and chastity can have only negative repercussions. And in the case of the Catholic Church, it made women hard, cold, callous, lacking in compassion, and drove men into sexual perversion and deviancy!

The wonder of it all is that the walls actually stayed up for so long!

Epilogue

The Catholic Church in modern Ireland

How Ireland has changed! And changed in so many ways! Socially, culturally, politically and economically! Unrecognisable now from the poverty-stricken, repressed and suppressed society that we have looked at earlier in this book!

We have seen just how *'Irish'* and *'Catholic'* became synonymous, first with the *'Romanising'* of the Catholic Church in Ireland by Cardinal Paul Cullen in the latter part of the 19th century, and then entrenched, fortified and bolstered up by Archbishop John Charles McQuaid in the middle decades of the 20th century. The power and control of the Catholic Church in Ireland, under McQuaid, was total, complete and absolute! At its zenith! All made possible because of the willingness of Eamon de Valera, himself a devout Catholic, and his Fianna Fail Government to hand over to the Catholic Church the responsibility for education, health and social welfare institutions in the new Irish Free State, and for establishing the moral fibre of the nation. New institutions funded by the State but run completely by the Church! Covering every aspect of people's lives! McQuaid, the control freak, with a finger in every pie! McQuaid who insisted that the Church and not the State should be the moral guardian of private morality!

But by the late 1970s, with McQuaid and de Valera both gone, dead and buried, Ireland began to experience *'change'* and no longer *'chains'*. And now? - Abortion, contraception, divorce, mixed marriages, gay marriage, all previously prohibited by the Catholic Church, - all now part of Irish reality.

We considered too, the visits of two popes to our shores, each visit a barometer of the nation's moral fibre, a barometer of Irish Catholicism. But how each visit differed! The first visit, by Pope John Paul in 1979 remarkable and notable for the vast numbers of people who turned out to greet '*Il Papa*', the second visit, that of Pope Francis in 2018 notable for the vast numbers of people who did not bother to turn out.

Pope John Paul's words to the vast crowds in front of him, words delivered just exactly one month after Louis Mountbatten was killed at Mullaghmore, County Sligo by the Provisional IRA, at the height of the Troubles in Ireland:

'On my knees, I beg you to turn away from the path of violence and return to the ways of peace.'

But the Troubles continued, even intensified. A clear indication, surely, of the waning power of the Catholic Church in Ireland!

And at Ballybrit? - *'Young people of Ireland, I love you!'* And warning the *'dear young people of Ireland'* against *'moral sickness'* - the challenges of more freedom from rules, the pleasures and attraction of materialism and the dangers of losing the traditional moral values of previous generations. And the *'dear young people'* gathered in front of him responded with resounding, ongoing roars, resounding ongoing roars that we all thought at the time were meant for John Paul himself! What adulation! What adoration! What exaltation! And the Irish hierarchy in attendance looking like the proverbial cats with the cream! They too, surprised no doubt at this enormous response from Ireland's *'dear young people'*! What a great idea indeed to have brought Pope John Paul to Ireland!

But Fintan O'Toole, in his book '*We don't Know Ourselves - A Personal History of Ireland Since 1958',* published in 2021, has put a different interpretation on this! O'Toole suggests that the thunderous wave of noise that rolled around the Ballybrit racecourse at Galway, when John Paul spoke those words, - *'Young people of Ireland, I love you!',* - echoing from one side to the other and gathering force and momentum as it went, intensifying every time the pope raised his hand to acknowledge it, - this could all be looked upon in another way. It went on for fourteen minutes, until Father Michael Cleary intervened to quieten them by saying, *'The Holy Father has not finished his sermon'*.

And how does O'Toole interpret all this? All this that looked like adulation! All this that seemed at the time to be an unstoppable torrent of sound and exaltation, in response to the pope's words! It was only looking back at the film afterwards that O'Toole grasped what was going on during those fourteen minutes. And instead of it being a show of religious reverence, *'that would reanimate Catholic Ireland for a whole new generation'*, it was, in fact, *'outrageously irreverent'*. The crowd, according to O'Toole, was not revelling in *'piety'*, but *'in itself, in its own youth and energy and unbounded vigour. It was taking over, inserting itself into the event, insisting on its own anarchic presence. It did not know or care about what it was actually doing: shutting the pope up'*. (*'We don't Know Ourselves - A Personal History of Ireland Since 1958'*, Fintan O'Toole, page 289)

That resounding wave that had just reverberated around the entire racecourse was, according to O'Toole, *'entirely of their own devising. The pope was helpless, powerless. He had lost control. He had been rendered speechless. This deluge of noise was filling the space where his stern sermon was supposed to be'*.

In other words, the *'dear young people'* of Ireland were having none of Pope John Paul's return to conservative Catholic Church control! The *'chains'* were broken, and *'change'* was unstoppable! Change that began in the 1960s. And these *'dear young people of Ireland'* were part of that change, - a new generation, intent on forging their own way. A new generation who knew about abortion, condoms, birth control and tampons, and who were already breaking away from paralysing, suffocating traditional values. And they were not for turning! Pope or no pope! John Paul or no John Paul!

Economic *'change'* in Ireland was giving these young people salaries, as wealth previously based on farms and land ownership was giving way to wealth based on professional qualifications and white-collar jobs. The Irish younger generation, unlike their predecessors, were educated and highly trained and skilled in technological advances. And those who had been the *'untouchables'* in the previous Ireland, - the Church hierarchy and politicians, - were no longer in that elevated position. And being in that elevated position, revered and respected had made them arrogant and unbending.

And just as in the early 1920s, where it was *'Brits out, Catholic Church in',* so now too, it was a case of *'Catholic Church out, capitalism in*!' And capitalism, with its economic boom, lured young people away from the Catholic Church. Despite the Catholic Church hierarchy fighting back! The newly-appointed Cardinal Sean Brady in a speech delivered at Knock on 17th August 2007, warned of the dangers of this new Ireland, a new Ireland of *'stocks and shares',* claiming that the shackles and chains of religious faith from which many believed they were now free, had only been replaced by the *'real captivities'* of the *'new'* Ireland. And this *'real captivity'* of the secular project in Ireland did not bring happiness, simply because of its failure to address the really important issues of people's lives. So spoke Cardinal Sean Brady!

But it was not just the young people who were drifting away! Many of the older generation too were leaving, having had enough, an over-dose indeed, of the horrifying clerical sex abuse scandals, the horrifying scandals of the Magdalene Institutions and the horrifying revelations that the hierarchy had been covering everything up. To many the Catholic Church has become just another corrupt, irrelevant institution, away from which people, young and old, are moving in droves! In fact modern Ireland could aptly be best described as *'post-Catholic Ireland'!*

And even though Ireland has indeed changed dramatically, - economically, culturally, politically and socially, - many aspects of Irish Catholicism remain largely unchanged. What has continued is the downward spiral of attendance at religious church services and the downward spiral of religious vocations, both to the priesthood and to religious orders. Continuing too is the adherence to the Catholic Church initiations of First Communion, Confirmation and the Last Rites. And some still attend mass on Saturday evening or Sunday morning, the Lenten Holy Week services, Christmas Day with children visiting the crib, travelling to Knock or other religious sites, and in the spring and summer of 2001, when the relics of St. Therese of Lisieux were brought to Ireland, huge crowds turned out.

But the numbers are very small in **comparison** to what they were in the mid 20th century. The **relative** decreasing numbers of Church goers and decreasing vocations, together with an ageing clerical population, - certainly does not bode well for a waning Church! A waning Church grappling today to retain what was once Catholic Ireland! A waning Church where those who still attend mass and Church services perhaps do so out of habit more than faith.

It is indeed both ironic and paradoxical that the same very rigid and unyielding conservatism that once gave the Catholic Church in Ireland its power, has become the cause of its ultimate downfall!

And why? Simply because change is the one constant in life! Ironic and paradoxical! And a Catholic Church that is set against and refuges to change in such a rapidly changing world as that in which we now find ourselves, cannot possibly survive! And today, as long-standing institutions continue to disintegrate in free fall all around us, for how much longer can the Catholic Church, in its present and erst-while form of institutionalised religion, continue to even exist, never mind flourish and prosper? And all this in the face of an influx of immigrants, from all different countries, all with different religious backgrounds and beliefs, coming into our country! All continuously changing the social, cultural, economic and political face of Ireland! The '*old Ireland*' dead and gone! Summed up in the circulating joke that it was impossible to find an Irish barman any more!

It all makes the conservative, draconian Catholic Church seem obsolete, outdated, outmoded, out of touch and out of fashion!

And the Catholic Church, like so many other great institutions, has fallen from within! '*The enemy within*'! - Much more dangerous than the enemy from outside! The enemy from outside you can see! But the enemy within works in covert, secretive, cunning ways! Like the enemies within the Catholic Church itself! - All those hypocritical, conniving, secretive child-abusing clerics, preaching one thing and acting another! And taking refuge behind their clerical collars! All those clerical hierarchy who covered up for them! All those members of religious orders who abused and tortured women and young innocent children in the Magdalene Institutions and in the Industrial Schools. They are the ones who have destroyed the respect of the laity for Catholic clergy. No more doffing of hats! No more stepping aside to let the priest or nun pass!

A great many people in Ireland still keep the faith, the *'faith of our fathers',* so we must ask, is it the walls of the Catholic Church that are tumbling down, or the faith itself? The walls of the draconian institutionalised Catholic Church, that kept the Irish nation in bondage and chains or so long? Has it just been a cult, with its elaborate spectacular ceremonies, its doctrines of the Immaculate Conception for example, its papal infallibility, its teachings on chastity and purity, its rehashing of the old Judaism/ Egyptian beliefs, - which has finally run out of oxygen? Just another scam? A scam based on instilling fear and guilt? A scam that made the Catholic Church the most wealthy institution in the world? A scam that promised Catholic Church members a pass into heaven, redemption and salvation if they obeyed the rules? A scam that fooled us all for so long?

Because no one, - no Jesus, no God, no Virgin Mary, - can **save** any none of us! Each one of us is responsible for our own Spiritual development and our own soul expansion. Each and every soul is meant to fly freely, not chained, caged or fettered! To fly freely and sing its own unique song, to contribute its own unique note in the overall harmony of the one great universal orchestra! And the Catholic Church, - with all its rigid codes of discipline, its stringent rules and regulations, its dictatorial control, its threats of hell and eternal damnation, its institutionalised hierarchal, patriarchal nature, - must, like all such institutions, all great civilisations, and all great controlling powers, as

And the Walls Came Tumbling Down!

history has shown, accept that with the passing of time, it too will **change** from the victor to the vanquished! Today the victor, tomorrow the vanquished! Today the victor, tomorrow the victim.

Let me now end with three well-known quotations!

First, the old nursery rhyme:

'Humpty Dumpty sat on the wall / Humpty Dumpty had a great fall / All the king's horses and all the king's men / Couldn't put Humpty together again.'

Second:

'There is nothing hidden that will not be revealed'.

And thirdly, Abraham Lincoln:

'You can fool some of the people all of time and all of the people some of the time, but you cannot fool all of the people all of the time.'

And so it is, so it has been, and so it will be!

Eileen McCourt

Bibliography

Arnold, Bruce - *'The Irish Gulag'*

Coogan, Tim Pat - *'Ireland in the twentieth century'*

Coogan, Tim Pat - *'Eamon de Valera - The Man Who Was Ireland'*

Cooney, John - *'John Charles McQuaid - Ruler of Catholic Ireland'*

Cullen, Clara and Margaret Ó hÓgartaigh, ed - *'His Grace is Displeased'* - Selected correspondence of John Charles McQuaid

Doherty, Gabriel and Keogh, Dermot - *'De Valera's Irelands'*

Ferriter, Diarmaid - *'The Transformation of Ireland 1900 -2000'*

Ferriter, Diarmaid - *'Judging Dev'*

Foster, R.F. - *'Modern Ireland 1600-1972'*

Hogan, Caelainn - *'Republic of Shame'*

Illingworth, Ruth - *'A 1950s Irish childhood'*

Inglis, Tom - *'Moral Monopoly'*

Joyce, James - *'The Dubliners'*

Kavanagh, Patrick - *'Tarry Flynn'*

Kenny, Mary - *'The Way We Were - Catholic Ireland since 1922'*

Kenny, Mary - *'Goodbye to Catholic Ireland'*

Keogh, Dermot; O'Shea, Finbar; Quinlan Carmel; - ed - *'Ireland - the Lost*

Decade in the 1950s'

Littleton, John, and Maher, Eamon - editors - *'Contemporary Catholicism in Ireland - A Critical Appraisal'*

O'Connor, Alison - *'A Message From Heaven - The Life and Crimes of Father Sean Fortune'*

O'Dowd, Niall - *'A New Ireland - How Europe's Most Conservative Country Became Its Most Liberal'*

O'Toole, Fintan - *'We Don't Know Ourselves - A Personal History of Ireland Since 1958'*

Phelan, Tom - *'We Were Rich And We Didn't Know It'*

Privilege, John - *'Michael Logue and the Catholic Church in Ireland, 1879-1925'*

Scally, Derek - *'The Best Catholics In The World'*

Other Books by Eileen McCourt

Eileen has written 49 other books, including her first audio-book. All are available on Amazon. For more information, visit her author page:

www.eileenmccourt.co.uk

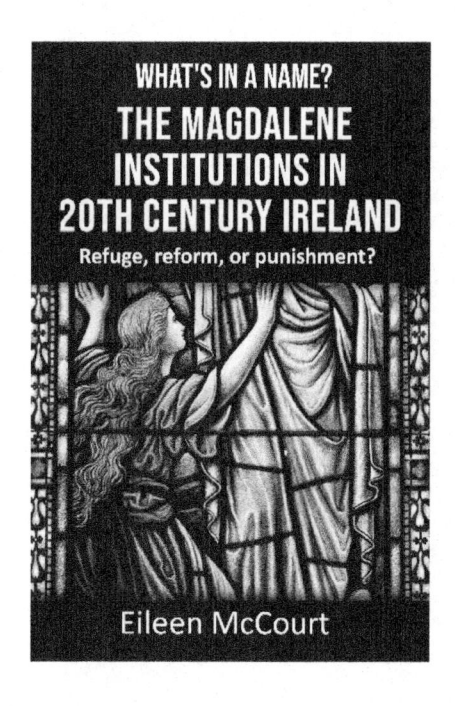

Other Books by Eileen McCourt

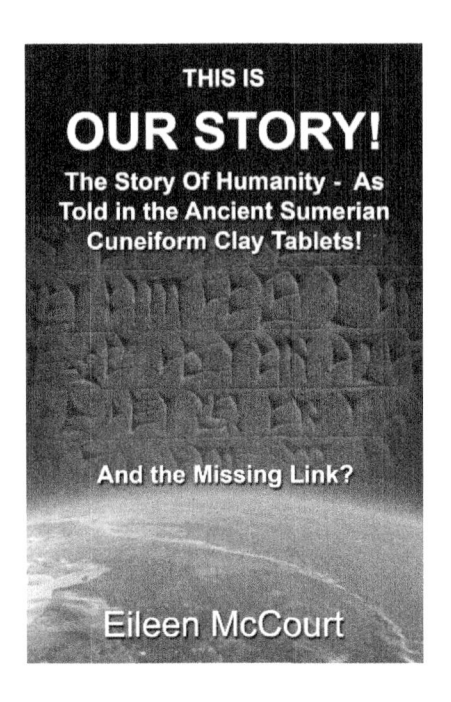

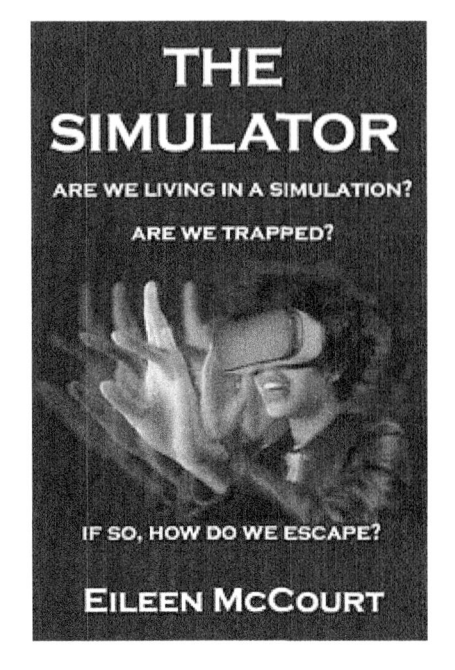

Other Books by Eileen McCourt

ANCIENT ANCESTORS CALLING!
With Wisdom and Knowledge for today's world
Eileen McCourt

LET ERIU REMEMBER!
Lessons and Teachings embedded in Myths and Legends of our Ancient Sacred Sites
Eileen McCourt

YOU'RE JUST A NUMBER! AND THE UNIVERSE HAS IT!
Encoded Within the Great Cosmic Code
The Magic Power, Strength and Significance of Numbers
Eileen McCourt

DEAR GOD... WHERE ARE YOU?
A Bewildered Soul Talks to God
Eileen McCourt

Other Books by Eileen McCourt

- Changing Your Life - Living the Reiki Way - In Today's World! "Just for Today..." Eileen McCourt
- ABOVE OUR HEADS! PREDATORS OR PROTECTORS? EXTRATERRESTRIALS! - THE BEST-KEPT SECRET NOW REVEALED? Eileen McCourt
- FINDING SENSE IN THE NON-SENSE Seeing The Greater Picture Eileen McCourt
- THE SINGING SOUL - THE RISE OF THE DIVINE FEMININE: THE POWER AND RELEVANCE OF MARY MAGDALENE IN TODAY'S WORLD' Eileen McCourt

Other Books by Eileen McCourt

LIVING EARTH
OUR RELATIONSHIP WITH MOTHER NATURE
EILEEN McCOURT

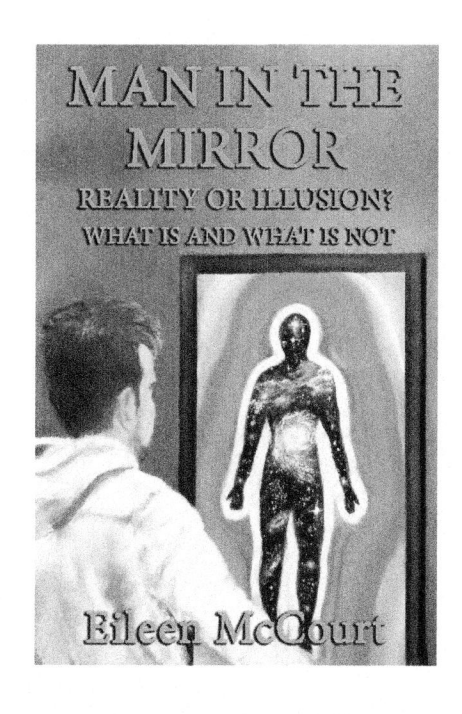

MAN IN THE MIRROR
REALITY OR ILLUSION?
WHAT IS AND WHAT IS NOT
Eileen McCourt

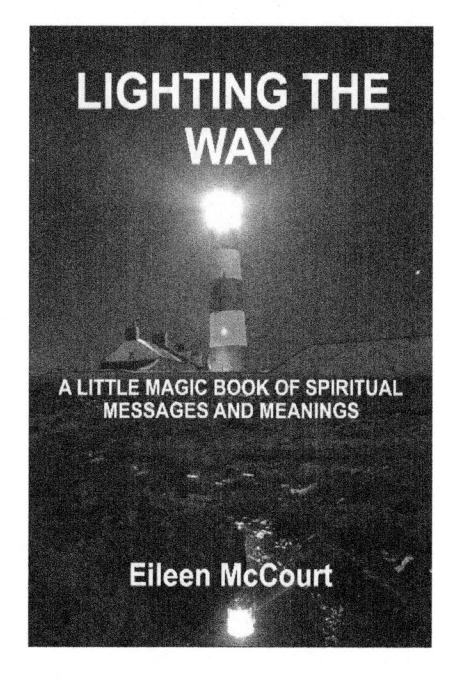

LIGHTING THE WAY
A LITTLE MAGIC BOOK OF SPIRITUAL MESSAGES AND MEANINGS
Eileen McCourt

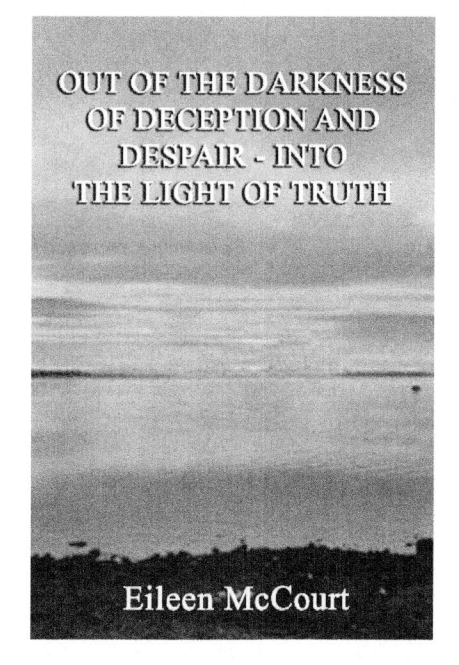

OUT OF THE DARKNESS OF DECEPTION AND DESPAIR - INTO THE LIGHT OF TRUTH
Eileen McCourt

Other Books by Eileen McCourt

Puppets on a String!
But! The strings have been broken! We are free!
Eileen McCourt

Humanity's Greatest Challenge?
Escaping out of the vortex of ignorance and superstition!
Eileen McCourt

Creating a New World
Nature WILL Be Obeyed - The Greatest Lesson Never Taught! But Which We Need To Learn
Eileen McCourt

What on Earth is Happening?
2020: Year of Balance: Rise of the Divine Feminine
Eileen McCourt

Other Books by Eileen McCourt

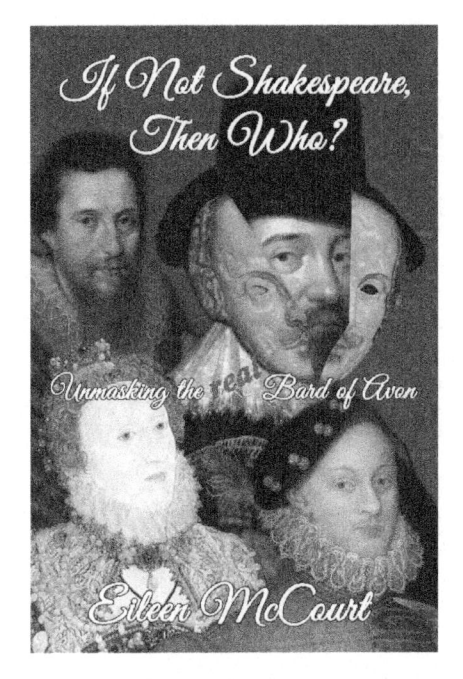

Other Books by Eileen McCourt

THOSE STRANGE LOOKING MEN IN THEIR FLYING MACHINES

VISITORS FROM BEYOND TIME & SPACE?
OR FROM PLANET EARTH?
ETs, UFOs AND WHO KNOWS WHAT

EILEEN McCOURT

HOMO SPACIENS

We Are Not From Planet Earth!
Our Connection With UFOs, ETs & Ancient Civilisations

Eileen McCourt

TITUS FLAVIUS JOSEPHUS

Author of the Gospels?

Eileen McCourt

THE TRUTH WILL SET YOU FREE...

CHRISTIANITY: WHERE DID IT ALL BEGIN?

Orion's Belt

Sirius

Eileen McCourt

Other Books by Eileen McCourt

Audiobook

Other Books by Eileen McCourt

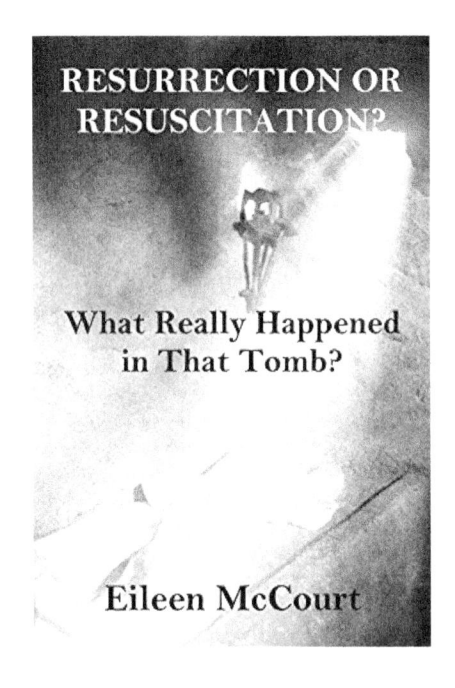

Other Books by Eileen McCourt

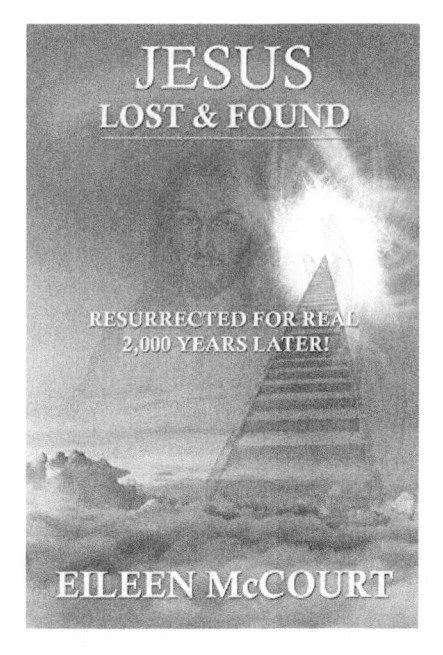

Other Books by Eileen McCourt

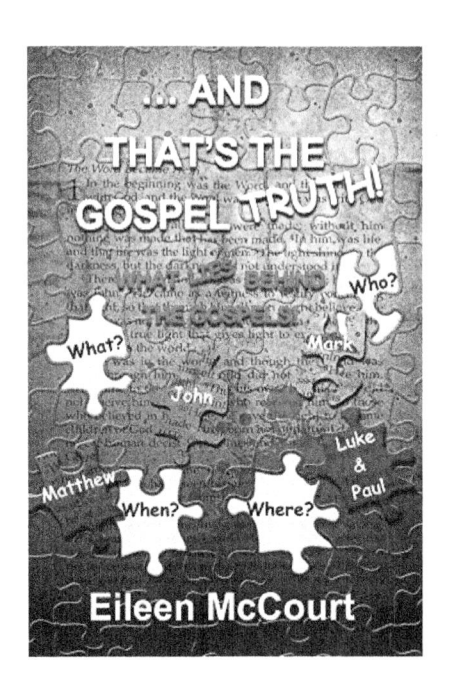

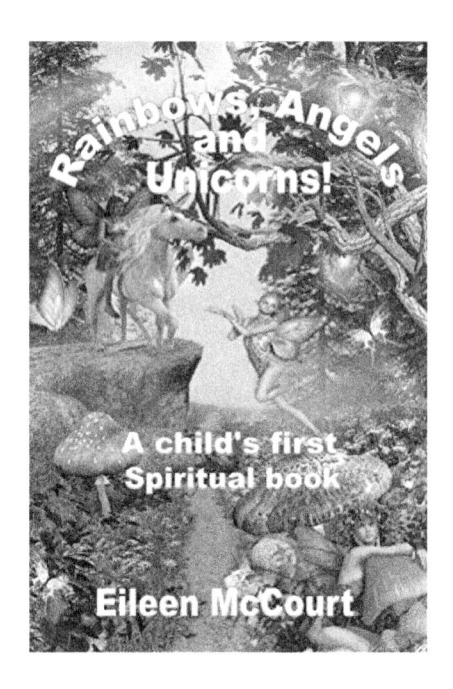

... AND THAT'S THE GOSPEL TRUTH!
WHAT LIES BEHIND THE GOSPELS?
Who? What? When? Where? Matthew, Mark, Luke & Paul, John
Eileen McCourt

Rainbows, Angels and Unicorns!
A child's first Spiritual book
Eileen McCourt

LIFE'S BUT A GAME!
GO WITH THE FLOW!
A Spiritual Manual for Today's Teenagers & Young Adults
Eileen McCourt

SPIRIT CALLING!
ARE YOU LISTENING?
Eileen McCourt

Other Books by Eileen McCourt

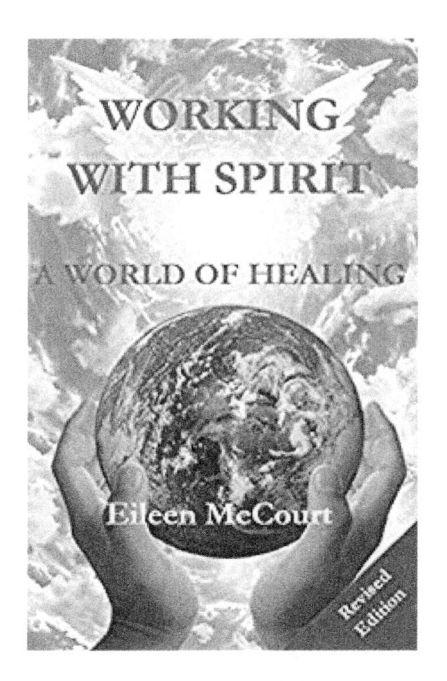

Printed in Great Britain
by Amazon